Hope you enjoy "The Ghost."
Merry Christmas!

Jack

11/22/09

My Father, "The Ghost"

My Father, "The Ghost"

The story of legendary still-busting Sheriff Franklin Smith

By
Jack D. Smith

Introduction by David Housel

E-BookTime, LLC
Montgomery, Alabama

My Father, "The Ghost"
The story of legendary still-busting Sheriff Franklin Smith

Introduction by David Housel
Book consultant, Angie Kiesling
Edited by Jody Naylor Sibley
Cover design by Al Eiland
Cover photo courtesy *The Moulton Advertiser*
Jim So's store photo courtesy Willard Vinson

Library of Congress Control Number: 2009938273

ISBN: 978-1-60862-095-1

First Edition
Published October 2009
E-BookTime, LLC
6598 Pumpkin Road
Montgomery, AL 36108
www.e-booktime.com

For

Patsy and *Wyckoff*
How can I ever thank you?

And for *Claire*...
a promise fulfilled. Here's your story, Angel.

Acknowledgments

I discovered right off the bat you don't write a book by yourself. It was a lot bigger job than I had imagined, but it would not have been possible without the people whose names you see here.

Patsy and Wyckoff Terry and Jerry Sibley head the list.

Patsy is my sister, Wyckoff her husband. With me two hundred miles away from where most of my research was centered, they hit the road, talked to people, and made phone calls – not to mention a gentle tug on my coattail if I had something wrong. Those two have memories that have dulled amazingly little over fifty years. What a joy it was to work with them on this project.

Talk about an encyclopedia of information, Jerry Sibley, who would be mayor of Mt. Hope if they had one, knows more about that community – and about my dad – than I ever dreamed possible. Many of the stories you see in this book emanated from his kitchen, sitting at the table over a glass of sweet tea at his second home in Auburn. Reba, his charming wife, made sure our glasses were filled and our food replenished. As you may know, Jerry has authored two great "Harley Earle" books. Aside from his content contributions for "The Ghost," he has guided me through the pitfalls of self-publishing. Without Jerry, Patsy, and Wyckoff I would not have even considered writing this book.

One of my great satisfactions is that the book became a family project in which my relatives, mostly cousins, joined enthusiastically to provide insight into Mom and Dad's life and to lead me to other resources. Cousins and their wives to whom I am forever indebted are Lanier and Jody Sibley, Don and Martha Sibley, Hal and Ann Sibley, and Horace and Helen Smith. I'm doubly indebted to Jody. She graciously agreed to edit this book, steered me away from grammar traps that I'm always falling into, and offered great advice on manuscript changes.

My cousin Horace Smith helped me find a lot of information on the early life of my father. I had vaguely recalled that my dad had some sort of accident when I was small, but until I talked with Horace I never knew he was in a coma and not expected to live. When I was growing up, Horace was an older cousin whom I idolized because of his athletic skills. I looked up to him then as a special person. I still do.

Thanks also to another relative, Edwin Smith, Dad's great nephew, who as a youngster made it a project to record some of the history of my dad's time in office. Some of what you see in this book came from Edwin's notes.

My Mt. Hope friends were great sources of information and inspiration: Dalton Reed, Ed Young, Elwyn and Melba Stephenson, Edward Allen, and Gene Pickens, among others.

Hayden Coffey, a valued friend of my dad's, provided a historical perspective that I could not get elsewhere – that and Mrs. Coffey's pecan pie. If I ever write another book I'm going to try to find some excuse to interview Hayden and Vaudie.

Myra Borden and the staff at Lawrence County Archives could not have been more helpful. Lawrence County can be proud of that facility and the people who work there.

The people at Decatur Public Library went all out to provide everything I asked for. Special thanks to Phyllis Roberts, who went up and down steps retrieving newspaper microfilm that was critical to my research. Thanks too to the good people at the magnificent Florence-Lauderdale Public Library. What a great resource for that town and county. My gratitude goes to the staff of Ralph Brown Draughon library at Auburn University, especially to those who handled newspaper microfilm, and to the staff in AU archives, who searched out old pictures to reflect the 1950s.

Harriet Bagby, clerk of the Birmingham office of the Northern District Court of Alabama, willingly plowed through massive files in the court offices to find fifty-year-old data and file numbers. Her work allowed me to find my dad's trial records in the National Archives. And it should be noted that the people I dealt with in the National Archives, from Washington, D.C., to Atlanta, were diligent and courteous in meeting my requests.

Harvey Elliott of Moulton, a former coroner and family friend who for years was owner and operator of Elliott Brown Service Funeral Home in Moulton, offered background information that allowed me to put into context much of the information I had uncovered. Cliff Bice of Auburn, a longtime friend and work colleague and an experienced communications administrator, offered suggestions and encouragement. He joined me in a visit to Mt. Meigs as we searched for clues to Screwdriver's identity. My thanks too to Wayne Booker, administrator of Institutional Services for the Alabama Department of Youth Services. He went above and beyond in explaining the life of Screwdriver at Mt. Meigs, including a tour of where Screwdriver lived and worked.

A first-time author needs a pro to lean on. That person turned out to be Angie Kiesling of Orlando, Florida. Angie has authored several books and edited a bunch more. She knows what's good and what's not and how to fix it if it needs fixing. She graciously agreed to look at "The Ghost." Her recommendations were of the type that caused you to think, *Why didn't I think of that?* Thanks, Angie. If I ever decide to write the great American novel you will be the first one I call.

Sheriff Gene Mitchell, himself a Mt. Hope resident, opened up the old jail and led my dad's four great-granddaughters and three grandchildren through the rusting cellblocks as they tried to imagine what it was like to live in a jail with prisoners as guests. Sheriff Mitchell struck me as having a lot of the traits of my dad, a soft heart for children, as evidenced by his interaction with my dad's young great-granddaughters on the jail tour, and a tough-as-nails crime fighter instinct. My dad's war was against moonshine. His is drugs. Thank you, sheriff.

Thanks to Bert Pippin and Ben Shelton for their help in searching for Screwdriver; to my best buddy in high school, Bobby Terry, who reminded me of long-forgotten stories; to Willard, son of Jim So Vinson, who provided background on Mt. Hope and a picture of the Vinson store; to high school and college classmate Steve Whitlow, retired ATF agent, for inside information on the workings of the moonshine business; to Deangelo McDaniel of *The Decatur Daily* for his advice and counsel on publication of the book; and to Ginger Grantham of *The Moulton Advertiser* for her support. *The Advertiser* and *The Decatur Daily* were the sources of much of the historical information in this book.

My thanks to the busiest sort-of-retired man I know, David Housel, who made time to write the finely crafted inspirational introduction for this book. You may remember David as the director of athletics at Auburn University or as one of the nation's top university sports information directors. I do too, but I knew him first as a journalist, one of the few whose writing comes alive with human emotion. You can see his artistry at work in the many books he has written and edited on Auburn athletics.

What you can say about Al Eiland is that he's among the best in his profession, a design artist with whom I have worked during my years at Auburn. Al spent several weekends and nights experimenting with a cover design that captured the essence of this book. I consider it a personal favor that he worked this project in and around his duties with the university. Al's resume includes work in Colorado Springs, Colorado, with Dr. James Dobson and Focus on the Family.

To Maggie and Claire Smith and to Reagan and Ruby Cunningham, my dad's great-granddaughters, go my love and appreciation. You were my inspiration. Special thanks to you for your valuable help in research and a great interview with Joyce White Peters. You elicited the information that formed the basis of the chapter titled "Our Own Little Miss Sunshine."

My gratitude to Dr. Dan Guin and his wife, Judy, of Auburn for their friendship and support during some of the darkest days of my life as I attempted to write this book following the death of my wife, Martha. Judy conducted grief counseling classes which I attended and which helped to bring some perspective back into my life. I will forever be grateful for her concern and for the compassionate and skillful manner in which she helped lead me toward recovery.

And to the greatest golf partners this hacker could ever hope for. In addition to Dan, these Saturday morning regulars kept pushing me to finish the book, knowing I was laboring with a heavy heart. Joe Judkins, Drayton Henderson, and Jamie Wilson deserve a little of the credit, or blame, for the work you're reading now.

I reaffirm my love and deep appreciation to Martha's family for their support and encouragement from the time this project began. Martha's sister, Betty Sue Shelton Smith, was a stalwart in assuming responsibilities created by Martha's death, thereby freeing me to concentrate on the book. I don't know what I would have done without her help, and that of Martha's and my niece, Jenny McAlister, and my daughter-in-law Lynn. Martha's sister, Jeanne Hurst, provided tips on sources that yielded information that ended up in this book. And I would be remiss if I did not mention, and thank, the world's greatest mother-in-law, Martha's mother, Hilda Shelton. As this is written, she is set to celebrate birthday number ninety-seven on October 23, 2009. That dear lady and I grieved a lot in our quiet moments together. She always supported my work on this project.

Finally, but not least, just two names: Mike and Lynn. You know what you mean to me. You and your two daughters are precious beyond belief. How blessed I am to have your love and support.

Introduction

This book is a look at life, a look at a time all but forgotten for most of us, but still revered, treasured and remembered in our minds and in our hearts, a time when people mattered more than money and when compassion and caring sometimes mattered more than strict interpretation of the law.

Who and why would anyone want to send an 11-year-old boy to prison, put him behind bars, for stealing forty-seven cents. Could it have been because he was black? Yes, there was bad as well as good in these remembered times, but it was a time when the good far outnumbered the bad. Or so it seemed, and seems.

This is the story of a good man and a good sheriff, Franklin Smith of Lawrence County, Alabama, told in loving recollection by his son, Jack Smith, a good man, an honorable man and a gifted writer and researcher as well. It is the story of a time long ago, but we hope not so far away. Not so far away that the values and relationships that marked this time can't be recaptured and once again become the hallmark and paragon of life not only in the rural South, but all of America.

Jack writes of a time that Margaret Mitchell might say is *Gone With the Wind*, but we can remember – a time when a man's word was his bond and even a handshake was more than was needed, a time of simple values, simple actions and good strong results. A time of the human touch that cultivated and still cultivates empathy, understanding and care for our fellowman.

We can hope and we can dream. We can hope and we can dream that the best part of those times will return. Not all of those times, mind you – we wouldn't want them all to return, only the best part, the strongest parts, the parts that made us who and what we are today.

Jack Smith has done a good thing within these pages. He makes us laugh; at times he makes us want to cry, and at times we are left aghast at man's inhumanity to man, but in the end we find comfort in the human spirit, that it prevails once again.

By recording these lives, these stories, he has reminded us, our children and our children's children of a time that was. And a time that could be again, if we would but live the right kinds of lives with the right kind of values, do the right thing and care for one another as we, as a people and community, once did.

Good book. Good read. A valuable addition to Alabama history, law enforcement history and to the archives of men and women who have tried to live the right way and do the right things, and who are still examples to us all.

David Housel
Author, Lecturer
Retired Director of Athletics,
Auburn University

Contents

Foreword

A Son Remembers

Despite his small frame, he was a giant in my eyes, a man of old-school grit who was more than a little bullheaded when it came to wading into dangerous situations.

They called him "The Ghost."

He would rise from the mist to nab a moonshiner, or so goes the legend of Franklin Smith. He could smell an open jug of the homemade hooch a mile away. If that is not so, you'd have a hard time convincing the guy with the jug. He'd swig his liquid corn as he scanned every tree and bush that might be hiding The Ghost.

If you and your cohorts were running off a batch at your still deep in the hollows of the Bankhead National Forest, you'd keep your eyes peeled for any movement in the underbrush because The Ghost could emerge from the shadows at any moment and yell, "Halt, boys. You're under arrest!" Odds are he and his fellow moonshine raiders would have to chase you down. You knew that if you got caught making the stuff, you faced a year and a day in the state pen.

If you hauled it, you held your breath until you crossed the county line. An arrest meant you lost your car and faced jail time to boot.

The Ghost was obsessed with destroying every moonshine still in Lawrence County, Alabama.

That perception exists even today among those who remember him. "Oh, that Franklin Smith could put the axe to those moonshine stills," they'd say, or something like it. He served two terms as sheriff of Lawrence County, from January 1951 to January 1959.

Truth is, the sheriff and his deputies did a lot of law enforcement that had little to do with making, hauling, or selling moonshine. Arrest records during his time run the gamut of offenses from murder to loitering.

But it was the moonshine that made Franklin Smith a legend. A half-century later, stories of his exploits undoubtedly have grown with age. Many of them stem from his relentless, and often creative, drive to wipe out the devil brew in that rural Alabama county eighty miles north of Birmingham.

He commanded respect, and sometimes awe, during the years he wore a badge and even afterward. One young man who had heard the stories from his father was surprised to learn that the 5-foot-10 sheriff weighed no more than 160 pounds, with rocks in his pockets. "I had him pictured as about 6-foot-5 and 300 pounds," he said.

Parents used his name to quiet their unruly children. "You better behave or Franklin Smith will come get you."

Let there be no doubt, though, that he had his detractors, and plenty of them. For the criminal crowd in Lawrence County, especially those in the moonshine business, he was always Enemy No. 1. He was sued, unsuccessfully, five times by people who claimed he or his deputies violated their civil rights in making arrests.

There were notable exceptions. What many people don't know, and didn't know then, was the respect afforded him by the very people he put behind bars.

A former big-time bootlegger told my nephew, Todd Terry, a few years ago: "Your granddaddy put me in jail many a time. He always treated me with respect. I still miss that man."

I do too. To me, Franklin Smith was much more than a still buster.

He was my dad.

If he was bigger than life to lawbreakers, he was twice that to me. Despite his small frame, he was a giant in my eyes, a man of old-school grit who was more than a little bullheaded when it came to wading into dangerous situations. He had no fear. I worried constantly that he'd be stabbed by a crazed drunk or shot by some felon bent on revenge. My sister, now Patsy Terry, carried with her that same fear, as did my mother.

Over these past fifty years I've tried to get a clearer, more objective picture of this complex man, hard but soft, gentle but tough.

I saw him draw his pistol with the obvious intent to kill a man. He thought I was in danger. He didn't fire only because I, his nineteen-year-old son, stepped in front of the intended target.

It was the gentler side of my father, the man with a tender heart, who I want you to understand. He was a still buster, alright. But he was so much more.

I listened as he encouraged a young husband and wife to kiss and make up, laying before them the joys of family and children. It was just their luck that my dad and I had seen them slapping at each other in public.

He had an especially soft spot in his heart for children. He and my mother, who as you will see was a valuable partner in my father's career, practically adopted a precocious, ever-smiling eleven-year-old black boy who called himself Screwdriver. He had been brought to jail on a warrant for stealing from a store in his hometown of Courtland.

An adorable three-year-old redhead named Joyce White stayed with us so much that, like Screwdriver, we considered her a member of the family. She found it not one bit daunting that we lived on the first floor of the county jail.

Franklin Smith was viewed as a serious man, and he was most of the time. But those who knew him best will tell you he laughed easily and often, had a mischievous sense of humor, and could devise ingenious practical jokes with the best of them, often drafting me to do the dirty work while he assumed complete innocence.

So this is the man about whom I agreed to write a book. Was he the man I thought he was? Could I be objective? The fear of finding negative answers to those questions – aside from the work involved in research and writing – made me reluctant to take on what I knew would be a lengthy and time-consuming assignment. I was retired, trying to cope with the unexpected death of my wife, Martha. I was working on my golf game and piddling in the yard when the notion struck me, which wasn't often.

I knew too that writing a biography of my father fifty years later would not be easy. Much of it would have to be filtered through my own memories and through the recollections of my sister, Patsy, and her husband, Wyckoff. I would of course need to interview those now living who knew him and research records and published reports. But my fear was that it would become my story, or Patsy's, because out of necessity we would be the source of much of the information that no one else could provide. To tell his story with any intimacy we had to tell ours. I trust the reader will understand.

I thought of all those potential problems when my son, Michael, urged me again to write a book about his grandfather. He was but the latest of the extended Smith family members who had strongly hinted that I write about the man whose descendents, except for my sister and me, know him today only through stories and old pictures.

"Would you write the book," my son asked, "if Maggie and Claire agreed to help?" I suspected he was thinking the book would be good therapy, but he knew the chance to work with my two granddaughters would get me. He was right. The book did turn out to be great therapy, and working with Maggie and Claire on this project has been a highlight of my life.

Not only that, but I'd seen enough of their work to know they could really contribute. They agreed to help. The deal was sealed. I could not turn down this once-in-a-lifetime opportunity to work with my two angels.

Maggie, fifteen, a freshman at St. Pius High School in Atlanta, is well on her way to a career in writing if she chooses that profession. You will see her work in "Reflections . . ." on the back cover of this book.

Claire, twelve, and a seventh grade student at Immaculate Heart of Mary School in Atlanta, just kept coming up with great ideas, making suggestions, and asking probing questions. She's a thinker, that girl.

Their involvement, I hope, has given them an insight into the life and times of the special man who was their great-grandfather.

My hope also is that his other two great-granddaughters, Reagan and Ruby Cunningham, Patsy and Wyckoff's granddaughters, may also gain an appreciation for an ancestor they've heard so much about. Reagan, twelve, a seventh grade student at Riverhill School in Florence, Alabama, and a budding writer as well, joined Maggie and Claire in interviews and research, as did Reagan's sister, Ruby, six, a first grader at Riverhill.

My dad's only two grandsons, Todd Terry and my son, Michael, were too young to remember their grandfather before he died. Suzanne Terry Cunningham, his only granddaughter, was not yet born. (I can only imagine how he would've spoiled that girl!) This too is for them.

For others who happen across these pages, may you understand what a special man he was, to us and perhaps to you.

To the surprisingly large number of his friends and acquaintances who yet live, we invite you to enter again into the life and times of those days when an unknown carpenter-mason from a little community called Mt. Hope rose to lead perhaps the most intense moonshine war the county has ever seen, before or since.

For me, Patsy, and Wyckoff, these accounts mark closure for a long-held desire that we honor in some special way this man whom we knew so intimately, who shaped our lives, who died too young.

Chapter 1

Mt. Hope Roots

Nobody was surprised that he would buy a Jeep; it was only when he started plowing with it that folks began to raise eyebrows.

I can't remember when, or if, he told us – my mother, sister, and me – that he planned to run for sheriff. Nor did he tell many other people. He could have told Uncle Floyd, who later became a policeman, or Uncle Grady, who owned a cattle and dairy farm a couple of miles up the dirt road from us. He and Uncle Grady were especially close.

Well, I'm sure he told us, the family, at some point. It's just that he never made a big deal of it. It was a big deal to us. If he won, we'd have to move the twelve miles to Moulton, the county seat, take up residence in the county jail, move away from the best neighbors in the State of Alabama, and, maybe worst of all for my sister and me, leave our classmates at Mt. Hope School.

His decision to keep his plans to himself didn't sit well with some of his neighbors and friends, who thought, perhaps rightly so, that they should have been afforded the courtesy of a little advance notice.

The day before his candidacy was announced in the local weekly newspaper, my father worked all day helping a neighbor build a house. He never mentioned his plans to the neighbor nor to another neighbor who was also working with them that day. That ruffled some feathers. It took a while to regain the confidence of these two good men.

At that time, I'm sure he was doing what he thought best. I never heard him say, but in hindsight I believe he would have handled his announcement differently. Here was a former cotton farmer with a ninth grade education, now a mason and carpenter, who was a shrewd trader of tractors and cars. But he was not experienced in the subtle, and sometimes not so subtle, art of grassroots politics. He needed the people of his home community behind him in a race that few people believed he could win – this in a county known for its rough-and-tumble, down-and-dirty politics that over the years had chewed up and spat out many a good man.

We lived at the time in a little western Lawrence County community called Mt. Hope. A lot of folks now, including the U. S. Postal Service, call it Mount Hope. The "Mount" part never looked right to me. So if you will indulge me, we're going to stick with Mt. Hope. At any rate, the community of Mt. Hope was filled with mostly God-fearing people who would show up at your place to help build your new barn or bring you a mess of squash and butterbeans and sit a spell just to be friendly. They were, and are, good solid folks who embraced the same values of honesty and integrity as my dad.

I'm convinced that living with and among these people reinforced a set of values that helped my dad survive the trials and tribulations that would befall him during the latter part of his second term.

The way he approached his first campaign was pure Mt. Hope. Simple, honest, no pretense. His word might just as well have been chiseled in stone. He lived by it. His loyalty to his own principles, his friends, his family, and his faith was locked into his very being. If that sounds grandiose, so be it. That was the man I knew. None of those tightly held values were ever articulated by my father. You just knew. It did not have to be said.

Including whether you planned to run for sheriff.

At the time he entered the sheriff's race in the spring of 1950, he was thirty-eight years old, the second youngest of nine children. His parents, Walter and Maggie Smith, had moved to Mt. Hope from Texas in 1906 after buying eighty acres of what was then known as the Templeton Plantation. The house sat along Roberson Road, now County Road 23.

From left, Walter Smith, son Franklin, wife Maggie (holding their youngest daughter, Luberta) and daughters Janie and Nannie Lee.

The old log home of my father.

Union soldiers had commandeered the log house and barn as temporary headquarters during their march through north Alabama in 1863. If my parents were aware of that bit of history, they never mentioned it.

My father and all but two of the older children were born in that old home-place log house, believed to have been built in the 1840s. He attended County Line School, making the half-mile trip by foot or horseback. As did most other youngsters of the '20s and '30s – he was born July 7, 1911 – he worked in the surrounding fields, chopping cotton in the spring (to thin the just emerged plants), picking cotton by hand in the fall, and gathering corn in late summer. He'd shuck corn for the livestock and shell corn for the grist mill. Cornbread was a staple.

He and my mother, the former Ruby Williams, were married on May 29 at 2 p.m. in 1932 by the Rev. Tommie Kimbrough in his home near Russellville.

My father had developed carpentry skills as a young man, and after he married he built a small four-room home on the family farm. My sister and I were born in that little house, I in 1934 and she in 1937. The house was a few hundred feet from our center of commerce and trade, Jim So Vinson's store and grist mill. The little frame building with its lone gravity-fed gas pump sat at the corner of Roberson Road and State Highway 24. We later moved a quarter mile south to the old home that my dad grew up in, still plenty close to walk to the store with a dozen eggs to swap for sugar or baking soda. Mrs. Vinson – Lillie Ann – was always accommodating, even when we would ask her to "put it down" (charge it), which was often.

Jim So's store: center of our trade and commerce.

The old home-place house had history on its side but little else. It was pretty much the same as when my dad grew up there. My father's great-granddaughters may be appalled to learn that their ancestors lived in what might appear to be dire circumstances. But it was home, humble as it was.

It had but four rooms, counting the room across the dog trot. That room had ghosts as did the loft upstairs. You can argue with that if you wish, but as a youngster I would not dare go in either place unless somebody was holding my hand. My daddy used to tease me and offer me a quarter if I'd go into the "ghost" room by myself at night. No way. A crisp dollar bill wouldn't have been enough either.

Except for the haunted room, I loved that old house even though it had...

- No indoor plumbing
- No running water
- No telephone, no television
- No electricity
- No central heat and air
- No locks. Never locked a door. Didn't need to.

A city friend once suggested that we lived in another Mayberry.

Oh, no. If we'd had the conveniences enjoyed by Aunt Bee, Andy, and Opie, we'd have been doing back flips all the way down our dirt road to Jim So's store. The Taylors had a telephone, refrigerator, electric stove, indoor plumbing – everything that we dreamed we'd have one distant day.

In the late '40s I doubt my dad had thought seriously about running for sheriff, although that may have been another of his ideas that he kept to himself.

At the moment, on this Saturday afternoon in 1948, he is a long way from occupying the county's top law enforcement position. He is in downtown Mt. Hope, a special deputy hired to oust the rowdies from the little unincorporated north Alabama town.

That's him over there on the porch of Roy Whitman's store. Dad's pistol, a .38 revolver, is concealed. Shortly, he will amble up the street past the post office and Dukemanier's Merchandise and stick his head into Tommy Sibley's barbershop to say hi to Tommy and his customers, who wait for their fifty-cent haircut. He'll move on up to Ed Young's Grocery store to talk to the owner, who played basketball at

Auburn. Then he'll saunter around to the back of Whitman's store looking for a drunk as he pretends to watch blacksmith Jim Dukemanier hammer out a replacement part for a broken-down hay rake.

The town is crowded. It seems that everybody comes to town on Saturday, including a few rowdies. Most of the time the rowdies are drinking or drunk and seem bent on stirring up trouble. You can even find a crap game down close to Hugh Mitchell's old gin. A man named Bogee Bush makes the best homebrew in north Alabama on Fridays. It is for sale today. Pay Bogee $5 and he'll tell you where the jug is stashed, maybe over there between the lespedeza field and the corn patch. Bogee is a skilled purveyor of spirits. My dad hasn't yet figured out how to catch him in the act.

It is here that my dad develops a bit of acting technique that will later serve him well as the county's chief law enforcement officer. For those he suspects of drinking, he gets right up in their face, pretending not to hear very well, but he is in fact trying to see if they have liquor on their breath. Ed Young, now in his eighties, ran his store for seventeen years. Once my father started to work, he recalls, it took less than two weeks to make the town safe for women and children.

The word gets around. Don't go messing with the new hired gun. He later cleared the Saturday drunks and rowdies from the little town of Landersville, a few miles up the road.

The rural towns across Alabama are not much different from Mt. Hope on Saturday afternoons during these late 1940s. Farm workers want to celebrate, and coming to town on Saturday to hang out and drink is their way of winding down from a long week in the fields.

If you want to see the real people of Mt. Hope, people who make the community special, go up to Leonard Roberson's place for the soil conservation picnic under those big pecan trees. The sweet tea and barbecue, if not the speeches, will make your trip worthwhile.

Or go to another picnic, the community's annual Fourth of July celebration at the school, for music and speeches and ballgames and ice cream and stew and of course visiting. The real people of Mt. Hope will greet you and make you feel at home. They will be at the school during basketball season too, when our purple- and gold-clad Yellow Jackets scrap it out with Hatton or Speake or Hazlewood or Lawrence County High, our rival in-county schools.

The real people of Mt. Hope would be at one of the town's five churches, and others nearby, on a Sunday morning and Sunday night, and for some, prayer meeting on Wednesday night.

Among them would be our neighbors along or near Roberson Road: the Sibleys, Spruells, Steeles, Millers, Gastons, Smiths, Robersons, Vinsons, Atwoods, and others. They were always there for each other in time of need. My father, I'm convinced, was shaped in significant ways by this neighbor-helping-neighbor way of life in Mt. Hope.

Downtown Mt. Hope was three miles to the east. But we were proud to call ourselves Mt. Hopers, as were those to the north, east, and south of downtown. The school and churches cemented the community, but mostly it was the school.

Strong principals like Dodd Cox, beloved vocational agriculture teacher J. R. Hawkins, and teachers like Bessie Cowan made it easy to rally round the school, not just for athletics but for its willingness to take children from a rural community and shape them into responsible adults. My dad was first in line to help with school projects. Most memorable was the day he helped Mr. Cox restrain a rowdy drunk who had made his way to a school picnic. My dad and Mr. Cox had no use for drunks on school grounds. If you wanted to see my daddy's dander get up, just let a drunk get near children.

Our school did an excellent job preparing us for life, thanks to parents like my mom and dad. Many of us young people of that '40s era earned college degrees and enjoyed successful careers.

But until the school started helping shape our lives, we boys had skills that weren't necessarily going to prepare us for life after Mt. Hope. We knew how to milk a cow, bring in stove wood, chop and pick cotton, drive a tractor, throw a baseball, and bounce a basketball.

We could shoot marbles, sometimes for keeps, eat salted peanuts out of a bottle half full of RC Cola without choking, and go skinny dipping in the creek over at Jim Sibley's place. Like a lot of other kids in the rural South of the mid-1940s, we – boys and girls, but especially boys – were woefully ignorant of many of the so-called cultural niceties of life. But Miss Bessie taught us table manners in the fifth grade; she showed us how to set a table, how to use a fork, and how to use a napkin. She also taught us to respect authority. Sit down and shut up meant sit down and shut up. In junior high, Mrs. Cox opened our eyes to Picasso and Van Gogh and Da Vinci. I secretly thought the guy who drew the Phantom comic strip in the Sunday paper was better.

We didn't realize it then, and I'm sure my daddy didn't, but few places on earth were, or are, prettier than where we lived at Mt. Hope. To our south the last remnants of the Appalachian Mountain chain formed a natural skyline that would put to shame anything New York has to offer. The Roberson farm was nestled at the base of that mountain. One part of that chain we called Eckerberger Mountain, home of caves and the natural wonder of hardwood forests. Hickory trees were so numerous that filling your hickory nut sack wasn't even a challenge. I am sure that as a boy my dad spent many a Sunday afternoon exploring those mountains and gathering hickory nuts, as I did.

On our side of the mountain were fertile fields that produced cattle, corn, cotton, gardens, and the salt-of-the-earth people who tended them.

I was visiting my cousin, Horace Smith, and as we walked from his home a half mile from the foot of those mountains, I remarked how lucky he was to live in such a beautiful setting.

"I had never thought about it that way," he said. "The mountains have always been there, and I've always been here. And I just never thought about how beautiful they are."

And so it was with the rest of us who grew up there. Go back six decades later and God's handiwork is the first thing you notice.

Still, as blind as I was to the natural beauty of our community, I grew up there feeling we had the best of all worlds.

I still do.

And I wondered why in the world my dad wanted to move us to a jail.

* * *

In recent years I've tried to reach into the far corners of my mind, hoping I can hear the tone and substance of Dad's conversations at home. I can see him but I can't hear him, for some strange reason. I have tried to recall what he talked about when we were just sitting by the fire at night, or what he'd say when he came home from work, or what his words were when the family was around the breakfast table eating Mom's biscuits and sawmill gravy. The images are clear – I can see him at the head of the table, just to my left – but the memories of specific intimate conversations are hazy. It's frustrating, but after sixty years, perhaps understandable.

Other memories, however, are sharp. I *can* see him lighting a Lucky Strike, almost one after the other, with matches stored in the bib of his overalls to keep them dry. I can smell the tobacco, which I thought then was delightfully aromatic.

"Jackie, go down to Jim So's and get me a pack of Luckies," he'd say. I'd scoot off on my bicycle, and if I'd managed to save a nickel I might even buy a NeHi Orange or an RC.

I can see this. He is plowing late on this day with his red H Farmall tractor in the field near our house. I yell at him. The day is April 12, 1945. He shuts down the tractor motor, the better to hear me.

"Roosevelt is dead! Roosevelt is dead!" I yell as I tear across the freshly plowed field in bare feet.

I had heard the news of the president's death in Warm Springs, Georgia, on the radio, maybe on the Tom Mix program.

He listens for a minute and says to me without emotion, "He is?" He cranks the tractor and resumes his work. A cotton crop has to be planted.

I never knew him to particularly like music. He'd listen to the Grand Ole Opry, though he was not a big fan. Curiously, in the late '40s I recall one song that he was especially fond of: Patti Page's "How Much Is That Doggie in the Window?" It would play on the radio and he'd stop to listen, or he'd turn the volume up a bit when he heard it in the car.

He could turn from a hardworking, serious brick mason-carpenter to a fun-loving kid when something struck his fancy. He loved to play Rook with neighbors, and true to his personality he'd often "Shoot at the Moon," that is, bid to take all the tricks.

He relished snowfalls, loved to hunt rabbits in the snow, and he was particularly fond of snow ice cream. A snow at night meant he'd be rousting Patsy and me from bed early in the morning. He would grab a bowl and head outside to bring enough snow in to make snow cream. Mother would stir in the milk and flavoring and we would dig in – before breakfast. The snow cream was a treat, but sharing a special moment with him and Mom was the real treat for Patsy and me.

My dad got along well with the boys of our neighborhood. He'd tease them about their girls or want to know how they were doing in school.

Dan and Jerry Sibley were his favorites. Since they and their parents, Tommy and Velma, lived only a few hundred feet away, the boys were frequent visitors at our house.

Dan was older, so he and Dad were sort of buddies. But he wasn't immune to Dad's teasing.

Patsy recalled, "One night we had a horrible storm, and the Sibley family came to our house because we had a storm cellar. They had gotten out of bed so hurriedly that Dan put his overalls on backward. We never did figure out how he got them fastened on the back. Daddy never let him forget that. I guess if Daddy were alive today he would still be teasing Dan about his overalls."

Dan, even as the occasional target of teasing, was clearly Dad's favorite among the youngsters in the community. He rode with our family to basketball games at Mt. Hope High School where we both played on the team.

"Mr. Franklin was a real close friend of mine while I was growing up," said Dan, now the owner of a NASCAR memorabilia store in Columbus, Mississippi. "He would always take up time with me. I will always remember how well he treated me. He was like a second father."

Like the rest of our neighbors, Dan was intrigued by the vehicles my dad was always buying and selling. He came home one day with a little Crosley station wagon with an engine that sounded like a sewing machine and was almost as powerful. Then came a Dodge truck, Ford cars, Farmall tractors, and a surplus army Jeep.

Nobody was surprised that he'd buy a Jeep; it was only when he started plowing with it that folks began to raise eyebrows.

"I thought the Jeep was the greatest vehicle I had ever seen," said Dan. "Then he hooked a disc to it and started plowing."

Jerry was a frequent visitor on his bicycle. Dad would be sitting on the front porch in the swing. This same repartee time after time:

"Franklin," Jerry would say, sitting astride his bike as he leaned against the front porch, "y'all coming up to the house a while tonight?"

"No," my dad would say, "I'm going to the picture show over at Muck City."

Total nonsense. Muck City, a wide spot in the road between Mt. Hope and Moulton, didn't have a theater. (Ironically, somebody did install a drive-in there years later.) But both my dad and Jerry enjoyed the banter, even if it was pure gibberish. That playful side of my father, especially in his interaction with kids, was a trait few people were ever aware of, especially after he became sheriff.

I saw him get really mad at me only once. I was working in the fields not far from the house, probably trying to thin cotton with a dull hoe. Chopping cotton was my least favorite farm chore. Mr. Woods, the mail carrier, came along in his '39 black Ford to save me with a card from church asking that I memorize the text on the card and recite it at church on Sunday. So I told Daddy I needed to spend the rest of the afternoon memorizing the card. I failed to mention that it had but one short paragraph.

"Well, since it's for the church I guess you can go on to the house."

And I did, with the honest intention of memorizing that card, except that other things kept interfering.

When my time came in church, and when I reached into my pocket, pulled out the card, and read it, I could see fire shooting from my dad's eyes ten pews back. Now, I don't remember exactly what happened when I got home, but I don't think it was pleasant.

It seemed he never quit working. I was about ten. The day was July 4 and he decided I needed to help him "drop soda" around the corn in the field down behind the barn.

I reminded him that July 4 was a national holiday, certainly not a day to work, so I'd just stay at the house and read my new Superman comic book if it was alright with him. It was not alright.

"Get your bucket, boy. We're going to the field."

So I sullenly went up and down those cornrows slinging handfuls of sodium phosphate fertilizer at the base of each stalk, hitting my mark every now and then, feeling sorry for myself, muttering – just out of earshot – how terrible it was that daddies subjected their sons to slave labor. As I recall, we made a good corn crop that year.

Five years earlier, he had survived an almost tragic accident.

He was working at a sawmill near his brother Grady's farm when a worker dropped a two-by-four on a moving belt. The piece of lumber flew into my father's head, knocking him unconscious. He was in a hospital at Russellville for two months, most of that time in a coma. He was not expected to live. Thank God, he did. How would my mom, armed with no more than homemaker skills, have provided for her two small children without him?

That incident was just another example of how, when things were happening, good or bad, my dad always had a knack for being right in the middle of them. And that knack seems to have followed him throughout his life.

In May of 1949, Dad was installing rafters on the new sanctuary of Mt. Hope Baptist Church, for which he served as a deacon. He looked down to see the men of two feuding families cursing each other and brandishing pistols and rifles just outside a nearby store. He jumped down, got in the middle of them, calmed them down, and sent them on. For at least a while a crisis had been averted. I doubt that his own danger ever crossed his mind. The previous sanctuary, itself newly constructed, had burned when struck by lightning. My dad's carpentry tools, a big investment for him at the time, were destroyed in the fire.

The last five years of the decade of the '40s were special times in our lives, and though the loss of our church hurt, the community – people of all faiths – came together to build a new one, even larger, even nicer. Why not? It was a time of optimism, a time of transition in our lives.

The clouds had parted from the dark days of war, those scary years when we sat transfixed before the battery-powered Silvertone radio as Gabriel Heatter and H. V. Kaltenborn carried us into battle with the Allied troops as they stormed Normandy, or put us in the cockpit of Allied bombers as they unloaded on Japanese-held islands in the Pacific. No longer would we have to worry about strange places like Anzio or Sicily or Iwo Jima or Guadalcanal.

A new era had begun and with it a new sense of hope.

That feeling manifested itself in many forms. Like in early spring when I would awaken to the faint but reassuring sounds of tractors in distant fields preparing the community's rich farmland for the soon-to-be-planted cotton crops. All was right with the world again.

The reassuring sounds of fall meant money, specifically when those sounds could be traced to the community's two cotton gins. We would sit on our front porch on fall nights and hear the roars of the gins three miles away in Mt. Hope as their whirling spindles snatched the fluffy white fiber from the seed. We would picture the line of pickup trucks and mule-drawn wagons loaded with 1,500 pounds of handpicked cotton waiting their turn to get under the swinging 18-inch-diameter vacuum cylinder that would noisily suck their cotton into the innards of the gin. We could see in our minds the gin spitting out a 500-pound bale every six minutes. We lived in cotton country. We knew the sound. We knew the process.

All but unnoticed came signs that life in our little corner of the world would soon be changing. A few new industries were popping up in nearby economic hubs like Decatur, Florence, and Huntsville, providing jobs to people whose experience had been driving tractors and planting cotton and gathering corn.

The bustling Saturdays at Mt. Hope, the roar of the cotton gins, and perhaps most importantly the deep-rooted traditions of small-farm families who depended on King Cotton to pay the bills and send the kids to school – they lulled us into a sense that our world as we knew it was secure.

But in the coming years, downtown Mt. Hope would be practically isolated on a Saturday afternoon. A special deputy to keep order was the last thing the merchants needed. They had gone too. The gins would slow to silence, eventually rusting into cobweb-infested relics. All this didn't happen overnight. Nor was it peculiar to Mt. Hope. Rural communities throughout America and the families who lived in them struggled to adapt to a post-war economy.

My dad felt these shifting winds of change in the late '40s. He didn't like what they portended.

His first move was to quit farming. He knew he'd never be able to make a better life for himself and his family with a little acreage devoted to cotton, corn, and a few cows. He seriously thought about buying a larger place to better compete with the big operators, even started negotiating a price. In the end the price was too high, the uncertain future of farming too great.

It could not have been an easy decision. He was a farmer at heart, a man of the soil who relished seeing crops grow. A white field of cotton was his Picasso, head-high stalks of green corn waving in the breeze his Van Gogh. He seemed never to be happier than when he was on horseback, or working with livestock, or taking off to the back forty with one of his beloved bulldogs, Bulger or Sport, at his side.

Patsy with Bulger.

That life ended around 1947. He traded his plow for a trowel and handsaw.

My father in his 1949 work clothes.

He could lay brick or concrete block so straight they looked like a painted picture. He took pride in perfection. His carpentry was square and true. His uniform was blue pinstripe overalls with big pockets that held his hammer, pencil, tape measure, and other tools of the trade.

He left his mark on Mt. Hope. Today, buildings he constructed are standing strong all over the community.

He often drafted me to mix his mortar, or "mud" as he called it. I did not like that job. You just couldn't satisfy that man, the perfectionist. "Mud's too thin, Jackie. Mud's too thick, Jackie." And on it went all day. I would've quit if I had had the option. I did finally start working as a clerk in Roy Whitman's store. Roy was a much better boss than my dad, and he was well stocked with RCs and salted peanuts.

I think what got Dad to thinking about running for sheriff was the special deputy experience. He knew that illegal liquor was rampant and that folks were fed up with it. He had a campaign issue, and people had begun talking about his no-nonsense approach to tackling the Mt. Hope and Landersville problems.

Then again, it might just have been in his blood. His older brother, Floyd, was a policeman and deputy. His father, Walter, was a constable who died of a heart attack in 1939 while chasing a burglary suspect.

He said none of these things, at least not to me or anybody I knew.

Folks in Mt. Hope and around Lawrence County learned of his intentions in *The Moulton Advertiser* on February 9, 1950: "Franklin Smith Qualifies in Race for Sheriff."

Chapter 2

Road to Jail

Could it be possible that we would actually be moving into the bottom floor of that new three-story brick jail they were building in Moulton?

By the time my father started his campaign for sheriff in February of 1950, we had moved into a new brick home within walking distance of Roy Whitman's store. Not quite in downtown Mt. Hope, but close.

It wasn't a big house; it had three bedrooms, dining room, living room, one bath, and kitchen. My father had mostly built the red brick house himself.

Nice, but I left my heart at the old log house on Roberson Road.

I missed the fig tree and apple tree out front and the hyacinths that bloomed purple and aromatic in the front yard. And the big rocks around the barn from which you, as the Durango Kid, could leap from one to the other, firing your cap pistol at mean old outlaws.

I missed the wooded lot behind the barn, where I occasionally hunted squirrels. And I missed the high roof on the old house that I could throw a ball onto, and as a filled stadium roared in awe, I would make amazing diving catches just before the ball hit the ground. I won many a game with those sensational grabs. My name was Lou Boudreau of the Cleveland Indians.

I even sort of missed the stubborn old cocklebur-tailed cow that I reluctantly had to milk twice a day, and I sure did miss Jim So's store and the gathering of friends there for RCs and salted peanuts.

Would I ever see Dan's daredevil stunts on a bicycle again, like the time he rode his bicycle off the back of a truck parked at Jim So's store? He would pedal fast enough from the rear of the truck's cab to gather enough speed to fly gracefully off the back of the truck, or so he promised. He would land upright, of course, probably planning to extend both hands in the air in celebration of a feat well done, an Evel before there was a Knievel. He had not taken gravity into account nor the loose gravel in front of the store. Dan, a couple of years older than we were, rode off home with little damage except for torn clothes and a bruised ego.

I missed the nearness of my two best buddies, L. O. Roberson and Charles Sibley. I missed corncob battles with my cousins Don and Buddy (Hal) Sibley. And I missed the crisp fried chicken that their mother, Aunt Luberta, would put on the table with just-picked-from-the-garden sliced tomatoes and green beans, fried okra, mashed potatoes, onions, sweet iced tea – and coconut cake you'd kill for. I tried to make sure I was visiting around lunchtime.

Lanier, the third son born to Uncle Merrill and Aunt Luberta, came along later, so it's been only in recent years that I have also come to know and love him and his wife, Jody, as favorite relatives, just as Don and Martha and Hal and Ann were before them.

Uncle Merrill, a dairyman and one of the county's most influential farm leaders, in later years became more than just a favorite uncle. He was a friend who genuinely cared for you and your welfare.

"Now, when you come home [from Auburn], you come down here and we will just ride around and talk," he'd say. Sadly, I never did. His death tore a hole in my heart.

The new house at Mt. Hope took some getting used to. Like my own bedroom, and a bathroom that took just four steps to get to (a big improvement over the two-holer out back at the old house). And that heavy black phone that connected us to the world – if you could get Miss Minnie to quit talking to her sister in Town Creek long enough to let us use the party line. And hardwood floors, an electric stove, and a sure-to-goodness refrigerator. Patsy had her own bedroom, which she adorned with frilly girl stuff. Andy and Opie and Aunt Bee would've been proud. We sure were.

But then that sheriff thing was always in the background. Could it be possible that we would actually move into the bottom floor of that new three-story brick jail they were building in Moulton?

Probably not, but still, there was always the chance.

The Democratic primary wasn't until May 2, but the candidates, including my dad, started their campaigns in February. In Lawrence County, if you won the Democratic primary and the runoff, if there was one, you were in. Tantamount to election is what the pundits called it.

The rumor was that there was a real-life Republican in Mt. Hope and maybe one down around Hatton. We youngsters often argued as to whether that could actually be true. And if it was, what do you reckon a Republican looked like? Maybe something akin to a New Yorker, we opined, though we'd never knowingly seen a New Yorker either.

So the Democratic primary was it. No general election except for the national offices. Most folks in Lawrence County never thought of the primary as anything more than *the* election. You had to go one county over to Winston – the Free State of Winston, they called it – before you'd see more than three Republicans in one place. People of that county stuck with the Yankees in the Civil War. We never quite forgave them.

The first campaign move was to "announce." That usually came in the form of a story in the local newspaper, *The Moulton Advertiser.*

Here was my dad's official announcement, published in the Thursday, February 9, 1950, issue of *The Advertiser*:

I have qualified as a candidate for the sheriff of Lawrence County and solicit the help of all people. If I am fortunate enough to be elected, I will do my utmost in carrying out the following things:
1. To enforce the Prohibition law to the (fullest) capacity with all possible help.
2. To practice honesty during the entire term.
3. To serve political enemies as well as friends.
4. To keep all secrets given to me.
5. To practice fairness to all and partiality to none.
6. To furnish the greatest possible protection to families and individuals, especially at churches, schools and on the highways.

The story goes on to say that "Mr. Smith is a deacon in the Baptist Church at Mt. Hope, is married, and is the father of two children, a 15-year-old son [me] and a 12-year-old girl [Patsy]."

I am not surprised by any of that, nor am I surprised that he listed enforcement of Prohibition first on his list. That was his campaign. The county was clamoring for a sheriff to clamp down on moonshine liquor, which many people said had gotten out of control.

"You could see stills from the road," said Hayden Coffey, who now lives just south of Moulton. "I actually once saw stills every hundred yards as I drove by one spot in the county during the winter when leaves were gone." Coffey, then manager of the Black Warrior Wildlife Refuge in the Bankhead National Forest during my father's time as sheriff, became a close friend and confidant of my father.

The point about keeping a secret might seem odd, but that declaration was paramount, and it was one policy that helped him develop his still-busting reputation. Informants, and he had plenty of them, knew that what they told the sheriff would never be leaked. He would protect his sources at all costs.

He had two election opponents, Lester Reed, a longtime highly respected law enforcement officer who would later serve as a deputy on my father's staff, and Vernon Persall, thirty-nine, a World War II Navy veteran who had been a Moulton barber for the previous sixteen years.

Persall was regarded as the biggest threat. That turned out to be correct, though a lot of campaigning had to be finished before voters in the May 2 primary picked a winner.

My dad hit the highways and back roads of Lawrence County's 693 square miles handing out campaign cards and asking for votes, as did other local candidates, including Reed and Persall.

Knocking on doors of strangers was not a pleasant routine for my father, at least not at first. Later I think he enjoyed it, especially during his second campaign when he was considered a shoo-in for reelection. But house-to-house visits were a ritual in rural counties like Lawrence. My father was not one with an outgoing personality. He'd win you over with direct eye contact and a demeanor that sent the message: You can trust me. I keep my word.

"Hello, ma'am, I'm Franklin Smith and I'm running for sheriff and I sure would 'preciate you and your family's support," he'd typically say, handing her a card that asked for her "vote and influence."

"You gonna do something 'bout all them drunks running up and down the road in front of the house?" she'd ask typically. "We got a bootlegger not a mile from here that's running wide open. It ain't safe."

He would assure her he'd handle the liquor problem, prevalent at that time in so many communities of the county. He was sincere, and most times he'd leave a home after such a visit with her vote in his pocket, and probably her husband's too.

He would leave for the campaign trail early and come home late. It was a grind, not just for him but for the family too. If he'd had a good day, then conversation around the supper table was upbeat. A bad day, say in an area where support was lacking, would create a somber mood.

Rumors were rampant. Persall was picking up support in the Speake Community, we had heard, maybe even in Mt. Hope. An advertisement in *The Moulton Advertiser* was signed: "Mt. Hope friends of Vernon Persall." What was that all about? Lester Reed was so well-known from his previous law enforcement career that he was bound to get a lot of votes countywide.

And so it went. A rollercoaster ride. One day we couldn't lose. The next, we couldn't win.

Then came the political rallies in the month before the election. Schools and civic groups had long ago discovered a rally's money-making power. As a candidate you'd better show up. And if you couldn't, you'd better send your wife or a member of the family to stand in for you. You knew your opponents would be there. Moreover, not to show up would be a slap in the face to the people of that community. In all the rallies in his three campaigns, we believe my father only missed one. And my mother represented him at that one.

My dad hated those rallies, but like other candidates he couldn't say it out loud. He went and pretended to like it, smiled, shook hands, and asked how the wife and kids were doing.

And if they had an auction, which they often did, you'd better have your checkbook handy. The wife of the most influential man in the community has her famous caramel cake ready for the highest bidder. Would you let your opponent walk away with the cake? At the least you'd better buy something. And you'd better brag on the stew, which is the best since your mother made it for you as a kid, and you eat it like it really is. You have the same smiling response for their barbecue or fried chicken or whatever else is served.

Thankfully, the county Democratic committee finally – ten years later – discouraged auctions at political rallies. And in ensuing years the rallies themselves slowly faded away.

But in 1950 they were going strong. The crowds were large. Interest was high. There was money to be made by the sponsoring schools or organizations and votes to be harvested by the candidates.

Each candidate had his or her vote-for-me turn at the microphone. Few were accomplished speakers, including my father. But he'd hammer on the moonshine problem and talk about safe schools and churches and other of his "announcement" points. Not fancy oration, but his obvious sincerity made his remarks effective.

My father would prepare his speech points on a scratch pad. And once he'd gotten his routine down, he could pretty much use it at all stops.

The kickoff for his first political rally as a candidate was Thursday night, April 13, in Moulton, sponsored by the local Democratic Executive Committee itself. This one attracted all the local candidates, plus a congressman and a few other state office candidates or their representatives.

"Never in the history of our republic have we faced such serious problems," intoned U.S. Rep. Bob Jones of Huntsville. "In a world in which men are seeking to be architects of a great world, shadows are cast upon it." More than a few politicians have stolen those lines in the ensuing sixty years.

Jones invoked the name of the most revered character in Democratic politics, in Lawrence County and elsewhere: Franklin Delano Roosevelt, who had died just five years earlier. He talked about Roosevelt's Tennessee Valley Authority, which had brought new prosperity to the region, and of FDR's rural electrification program and pavement of rural roads. He knew how to push their buttons. Nearly everybody in that north Alabama county had benefited from one or more of those programs.

For many local candidates, pushing voter buttons had as much to do with personality as it did with character, experience, and issues. For my father though it was the issue. "Moonshine" in this year was absolutely a critical vote-changer.

The next night my dad and the other candidates headed off to Speake High School to do it all over again. Then to Town Creek on Saturday night, Hatton on Tuesday night, Landersville on the following Saturday night, and to Mt. Hope on the following Thursday night. And on it went.

Tuesday, May 2 – Election Day – couldn't come soon enough. Win or lose, let's get this campaign done with.

The day dawned warm and sunny but with a threat of thunderstorms later. Speculation was that a heavy turnout could mean that voters, fed up with rampant moonshine problems, would probably favor my dad. But who could tell?

From Red Bank and Loosier and Oakville and Morris Chapel and twenty-four other boxes would come results hand-delivered by poll officers to election officials at the courthouse in Moulton.

If this box or that box came in late, you would overhear in the waiting crowd, "They're stealing votes is what they're doing."

Nervous supporters of a particular candidate would latch onto every rumor, most of which were likely completely false. Still, stories abounded about the shenanigans spawned by the blood sport that was Lawrence County politics. No doubt some were true.

Who was Judge Johnson throwing his support to this time? Judge Isaac Johnson, a longtime probate judge, was a political power in the county. It was a question worth asking.

It was obvious from the first returns that dad would have a good night. But would he get enough to win without a runoff? This was Tuesday. He had to wait all the way to Saturday afternoon to learn for sure that he would be the next sheriff of Lawrence County.

Here's what happened. Poll workers in one of the big – 622 votes – Moulton boxes began squabbling. While county residents and my dad waited, the vote counters struggled along at a frustratingly slow pace. They had been counting, or trying to count, ballots for 36 hours, and they still weren't finished. At 6:30 Wednesday evening, one poll worker announced that he'd had enough and went home.

County Democratic Committee Chairman C. A. Young pleaded with the workers to finish the count. After all, they lacked only twenty-five or thirty ballots. No sir, they said, they'd counted long enough. The box was locked up for the night and officials spent Thursday trying to figure out what to do.

The Democratic Executive Committee decided to count the votes themselves – in the courthouse in front of whoever wanted to watch. They set up shop in the courtroom, surrounded by candidates and their supporters, who knew that results from that box would determine their fate.

My dad might have been a bit uneasy, but he had done enough figuring to know that he stood a good chance of winning without a runoff. But he didn't know for sure until Saturday afternoon when the Democratic committee announced the official results.

The final vote count was Smith, 2,647; Persall, 1,694; and Reed, 605. My dad received a majority with 89 votes to spare, so a runoff, mercifully, wasn't necessary. He had been anxious about the support he'd receive from his home community. He needn't have worried. The Mt. Hope box went to him 208 to 97 for the combined total of his two opponents.

Uh-oh! We're going to jail. The reality of it all set in.

We hated to leave our beloved Mt. Hope. But as time for our move inched toward January 19, 1951, the date my father would take office, our apprehension waned. Excitement rose, not just for my dad but for Mother, Patsy, and me as well.

We were all about to enter an exciting new phase of our lives. For me, the chance to play basketball and baseball for one of Alabama's most celebrated coaches, Grady Elmore, was a happy result. Outside of my own father, I respected and admired no man more. He never asked me to go out for football. There were two good reasons. I had never worn a football uniform in my life, and more importantly I probably didn't weigh 120 pounds soaking wet.

The rest of the family, Dad, Mom, and Patsy, wouldn't be moving until toward the end of the year. My sister stayed behind with her seventh grade classmates at Mt. Hope. She would join her new class at LCHS in January. But when the 1950-51 school year began in August, I enrolled at Lawrence County High School in Moulton. I was able to enroll at my new school thanks to a kindly "Star" route mail carrier who let me ride with him as he made runs each

51

morning and afternoon between the Moulton and Mt. Hope post offices.

Later I moved in with the Wallace family in Moulton two blocks from the school. Cecil and Mrs. Wallace and their children, Jimmy and Judy, were wonderful, warm-hearted, generous friends. And I will forever be grateful. I trust Jimmy did eventually learn to play the fiddle.

As time grew closer for the move to jail, my mother, father, and sister lived with the Wallaces too.

January 19 was dead ahead and coming fast.

A strange new world was upon us.

And it would change our lives forever.

Chapter 3

"The Ghost"

"He'd just appear out of thin air to make an arrest..."

My wife Martha and I were in Moulton visiting her mother and preparing to go to some event, maybe a wedding or wedding reception. It was something where you had to wear a tie and look nice and all. She decided I needed a haircut.

My seventy-one-year-old gray hair had gotten a bit shaggy, so I dutifully did as I was told and went to a nearly deserted downtown in search of a barber.

I spied a candy cane pole right next to the gap where Slim Hambrick's City Grill used to be. It was like somebody had knocked a tooth right out of the row of businesses. It hurt to see that. I had eaten many a good hamburger there in the early '50s, had taken my girl there, and put more nickels than I could afford into the jukebox and hummed along with Georgia Gibbs and Patti Page and Nat King Cole, and the one that really got my heart throbbing (and I hoped hers), Johnny Ray singing "Cry."

So I was in a melancholy mood on this day in 2005 when I stepped into the barbershop and sat down to await my turn. The lifeless downtown didn't help my feelings either. Moulton was no longer the bustling little town of my youth.

That's when Flynn Owen, owner of the shop, changed my attitude. He flashed a "come on in" smile and a "be with you in a minute" welcome that let me know the old hometown's hospitality was alive and well. But I knew that hidden behind that friendly smile was a voice saying, "Who in the world is this guy?"

When I told him I had lived in Auburn for the past forty-five years but that as a teen I had lived in the county jail at the back of his shop, he figured out I was Franklin Smith's son, which set off such remarks in the shop as "There'll never be another Franklin Smith" and "That Franklin Smith was something alright."

An older gentleman with white hair turned to me and said, "You know what they called your daddy, don't you?"

Well, no, not exactly.

"The Ghost," he said. "They called him 'The Ghost.' At least that's what the moonshine whiskey people called him. He'd just appear out of thin air to make an arrest – or it seemed that way – and you'd be headed for jail before you knew what happened."

He said he had been warned of The Ghost when he was a young man gallivanting around on a Saturday night looking for a little something to drink.

"Me and a buddy went down to a bootlegger and tried to buy a pint of moonshine," he remembered. "The bootlegger told me he had stashed a pint next to a certain gravestone down in a cemetery close to his house. He wouldn't get it for us; he said Franklin Smith might just step out of the bushes."

So he and his friend headed off down to the cemetery to claim their purchase.

"We circled around that gravestone a bunch of times, looking at the whiskey, afraid to pick it up. We finally grabbed it and chugalugged it down before The Ghost could get us. Franklin didn't catch us that night, but he sure made us nervous." He stopped the story there. I doubt that he could remember the rest of it.

Owen, listening to the story he obviously had heard before, said to me, "You ought to write a book about your dad. There's a whole lot of stories around like that."

"Well, maybe one day," I said, and let it go at that. But at the time I had no intention of writing a book. I was just hoping my haircut got you-know-who's stamp of approval. (It did.)

* * *

Franklin Smith's war on moonshine and his reputation as The Ghost had begun more than a half-century earlier on a rainy, cold January night in 1951 when he and our family moved into the first floor of the county jail. Well, it didn't start precisely on that night because that was the night we got acquainted with Junior.

We were just getting settled in, trying to figure out where everything was and getting familiar with the odor of commercial cleaning compounds used on the floors and walls and which big old jail key fit which big old jail door.

The phone rang, ominously. First call. A murder? Robbery?

My dad answered.

"They's a body in the ditch down here in Langtown," she said, giving him more specific information on exactly where the ditch was.

I jumped into the car with my dad, and we sped off to Langtown, a community five miles north of Moulton. Sure enough, there was the body, face down in a water-drenched ditch.

My dad turned him over. He was not dead. He was just dead drunk. We poured him into the backseat of the car, hauled him to jail, got him into some dry clothes, and laid him on a cell bunk to sleep it off.

We did not know it then, but Junior Sledge was to hold the record for most arrests during my dad's eight years in office. He was Mayberry's Otis, the difference being that he didn't come in and lock himself up.

The thing about Junior was he was just a good old boy who everybody liked, so it was hard to turn him down when he asked you for a dollar to get something to eat, even though you knew he'd probably buy something to drink instead. Often it was bay rum or rubbing alcohol. He'd been off to war and fought for his country and, well, why not cut this gentle soul a little slack?

My dad always did. He or a deputy would go get Junior, charge him with public drunkenness so the state would pay for his jail breakfast, then "nol-pros" the case, which meant the charge was not prosecuted.

There were an awful lot of nol-prosses beside Junior's name in the 1950s. What it boiled down to was that Junior's jail time was free room and board paid for by the state. My dad was fine with the free bed and breakfast. He just didn't want Junior to die in a wet ditch somewhere.

So Junior was my dad's first arrest as sheriff. And the only thing it had to do with moonshine was that Junior drank too much of it.

The still-busting war was to come soon, however.

It started with hiring the people on the front line, the deputies. I always thought my dad's first set of deputies was the best of his eight-year tenure.

Clarence "Hot Rod" Harris was the chief deputy with plenty of experience in law enforcement. He had a go-get-'em reputation. Theo Rucker was Dad's first cousin, ready to take on any challenge. Like my dad, he'd back off from nothing. Claude Lee Terry, from Courtland in the valley area near the Tennessee River, lacked experience but provided geographic balance and was highly respected as an honest and fair man. A small group but a good group.

Hot Rod (he liked that name, used it in one of his own campaigns later) was a small man, a little bigger than Barney of Mayberry, with none of Barney's timidity. His pistol hung low down his side, and I was sure that someday it would drag his pants down. I don't reckon it ever did. I figured he wore his sidearm that way as a sort of personal trademark.

Hot Rod and Dad had the same passion for wiping out moonshine, and the new chief deputy had plenty of experience in the art of finding stills. One thing about him was his amazingly sharp eyesight. Which is why I'd find myself occasionally driving slowly over mountain roads with Hot Rod as a passenger.

He would put his arms and head outside the passenger-side window, intently studying roadside ditches for the tiniest of signs that weeds or dirt had been disturbed. He was looking for places that corn mash and sugar, ingredients in whiskey manufacture, had been unloaded. A broken twig or bent blade of grass could mean a still was nearby.

So credit at least a few of those hundreds of stills axed in Lawrence County during the '50s to Hot Rod Harris' eagle eyes.

The unsung hero of the new sheriff's team never went on a still raid, or as far as I know ever arrested anybody.

She was my mother, and it was her job to keep the jail running smoothly, hire the cooks, plan the prisoners' menu, serve as the sheriff's secretary, and do just about anything else that needed doing. That included regular family stuff like keeping us all in clean clothes and getting Patsy and me off to school. Oh yes, she was an important part of that team, and my dad and the rest of us knew it.

The Lawrence County whiskey rebellion had other allies too. Two of my favorites were Carlos Nelson and Herman Sandlin. They were state Alabama Alcoholic

Beverage Control agents, and they were in on the majority of still raids in the county.

Other ABC agents sometimes joined the raiding party, as did federal Alcohol Tax Unit (ATU) agents, whose title later would become Alcohol Tax and Firearms agents (ATF). But Carlos and Herman were our favorites.

Occasionally, we were honored to have the legendary ATU agent Sam Posey take part in a raid, just the big ones though. His favorite tool of still destruction was dynamite. It was said that when he retired, the folks who cleaned out his office in Birmingham found enough dynamite to blow up half the city. He was the kind of man my dad admired.

Chapter 4

Lawrence Liquor – '50s Vintage

Why it's called moonshine: In the old days, distillers burned wood to heat the fermented mash, which made vapors that condensed into whiskey. Wood made smoke. Lawmen could see smoke in the daytime. So the moonshiners made whiskey at night by the light of the moon. Butane gas and oil were the fuels of choice in later years.

You can call the stuff wildcat or white lightning or mountain dew or corn squeezin's or hooch or rotgut or granny's special elixir and folks will know what you're talking about.

Whatever you called it, there was plenty of it when my dad moved into the sheriff's office. He could not have been elected at a more opportune time. Moonshine whiskey manufacturing in the United States had peaked in the 1950s, and Alabama and Georgia were the biggest culprits.

Of every five gallons of whiskey consumed in the United States during that time a full gallon – 20 percent – was illegally made moonshine. The illegal part was that the government didn't get any tax money from it, like say when you bought a fifth of Jack Daniels at the liquor store.

Lawrence County had two classes of moonshine makers and sellers. The first were the small timers, maybe farmers who'd run off a little on the side to help pay for family expenses. Industrial jobs had begun to open at nearby

Decatur and in the Florence-Muscle Shoals area. But those jobs had not yet made a big impact on the county's economy. They would later.

So moonshining was an attractive, if somewhat risky, way to add income for some small-acreage farmers. (In 1950, the county had 4,142 farms; by 2002 that number had dwindled to 2,074.) They would have a little 100-gallon still over in the back-40 woods. They were the ones who drank a little of it, sold a little, and gave away a little.

The second class, those my dad relished arresting, were the big operators, the kingpins who gathered in big money making moonshine and transporting it to markets such as Memphis and Birmingham and to smaller nearby towns like Decatur and Florence.

Estimates at that time were that a moonshiner could produce a gallon of whiskey for about a dollar, maybe two, and sell it for $8 or $10. He dealt in cash; no paper trail for the IRS. The big operators were way too smart for that. You'd usually find their stills along creeks in the hollows of the mountain region south of Moulton.

That was especially true of the 189,000-acre Bankhead National Forest, a large portion of which was in Lawrence County. They would run off hundreds of gallons of whiskey from big stills, the 2,000- or 3,000-gallon-capacity tanks that held the fermenting mash. And often three or four of the big stills were clustered along some hidden creek. Just one 1,500-gallon still could produce 150 gallons of whiskey a week, a federal ATU agent remarked once after joining the sheriff's force in a raid. At $8 a gallon, that much production from one still that held 1,500 gallons of mash would gross the moonshiner $1,200 or more – a huge weekly payoff in the 1950s.

Oftentimes moonshiners' cars would be equipped with high-powered engines, the better to outrun the law. A reworked '40 model Mercury was said to have been the car of choice. Its strong replacement springs would hold steady on tight turns and keep the car level even with 100 gallons of whiskey, often in 5-gallon metal GI cans or 5-gallon glass jugs, in what used to be the backseat. A low rear end was the lawman's best tipoff that a load of whiskey might be in the back. The big operators were usually the more skilled ones, both in making whiskey and evading the law, though a lot of the little distillers knew all the tricks too.

Lookouts spotted around a still site were common. But there were other techniques too. A thin, nearly invisible string would be placed across a trail. A broken string could mean a revenuer had been around. A twig placed in a roadway is broken. Caution: Somebody's been around here that's not supposed to be. A coin was sometimes placed on the edge of the cap covering the hole in the mash vat. If the coin has been moved or has fallen into the mash, the moonshiner can be pretty sure the law has been messing around the still, probably testing the mash to determine when it's ready to distill, which tells the officers when to plan a raid.

The bootleggers, those who sold it retail, mostly in pint bottles or quart jars, had their own set of tricks. And they confounded my father and his deputies more than once.

Like this bootlegger who for a while did a booming business. My father knew he sold whiskey, lots of it. He'd raid the home and premises. No liquor. Another raid. No liquor.

Finally, totally perplexed, my dad had a deputy drop him off near the man's house on a Saturday night, the most popular time for moonshine sales. He slipped into a wooded area and found a place from which to watch the house. He waited.

Soon cars began stopping for no more than a minute or two. He could see money change hands but no whiskey. He slipped down a tree line to watch where the cars were going.

What he saw was a practice that he later learned was a common tactic in bootlegging operations. On that night he watched as cars would stop, find a fence post, dig a pint of whiskey from its base, and move on.

The next weekend he made another raid at the house. No whiskey. Then dad asked the bootlegger to take a little walk with him. They went down a nearby row of fence posts, my dad picking up pints of whiskey. Next stop: jail.

Those who sold the stuff from their homes found ingenious ways to hide it from lawmen who came calling with a search warrant. False panels that hid the hooch were fairly common. But one of the best was an icebox with false sides that held many cans of beer. How the adapted icebox was discovered is lost to time, but it was confiscated and brought to the jail.

The local paper ran a picture of it, and people would drop by and ask to see the box.

Selling beer illegally in our dry county was a fairly common practice, according to lawmen of that era. The younger crowd would gladly pay double for a can of beer rather than drive twenty or thirty miles to Leighton in wet Colbert County or Madison in wet Madison County.

The in-home bootleggers were ahead of the curve when it came to marketing. Some of them had a drive-in window on their back porch or behind the house.

Drive up, ask for a Bud or Schlitz or Pabst Blue Ribbon or a Falstaff or Carling Black Label, and you might get the brand you wanted or you might not. Beer bootleggers sold beer. You took whatever brand they had. You could also ask for a "church key." In those days you had to have the "key" to punch a hole in the top of the beer can.

Now, I don't know for sure whether Lawrence County bootleggers had drive-in windows, but I suspect they did.

In these days when you can buy beer and gas at the same place, or groceries and wine in the same store, all this must appear archaic. It wasn't at that time. You had to have lived then to understand it.

The bootleggers were a ways down the moonshine production and marketing chain. At the top were those who made it. Then came the haulers, then the bootleggers, who in those days charged $2 a pint, and finally those who drank it.

Makers and haulers were often the same person. The kingpins were in that group. The bootleggers seldom partook of their product. Their motto: It was made to sell, not to drink. Among the drinkers were those who would drink anything they could afford, and moonshine was relatively cheap and – before the moonshine war began – readily available. Junior was in that group. The other drinkers just had a taste for moonshine and preferred it over anything else. Not too many in that group, but they did and still do exist.

The drinkers were reflected in arrest records as PDs – public drunkenness. They outnumbered the distilling and transporting and bootlegging charges maybe 10 to 1. Bootleggers were usually charged with violating the Prohibition law. Individuals were too if they had liquor, moonshine, or store-bought, or beer on them or in their car. Lawrence was a dry county in a legal sense only.

Occasionally, the state toxicologist would send out a news release urging folks not to drink moonshine because it could kill you, and not just from drinking too much of it.

Forty-five percent of moonshine tested contained potentially lethal deposits of lead, said one news release of that era. Three percent contained deadly wood alcohol.

The lead would often come from old vehicle radiators used as condensers. Lead could and did kill a goodly number of moonshine drinkers, and it made some of them blind. The smart drinkers, if there were such beings, tried to stay away from "radiator likker."

Law enforcement officers were mainly interested that the stuff contained alcohol. That made it illegal. They were not all that worried about the unsanitary conditions under which it was made. They can tell you some appetite-killing stories, though, about all the stuff they've found in Lawrence-made liquor.

I watched as deputies brought in a load of wildcat whiskey one afternoon that was reeking with saturated bugs. It was not uncommon for a stray dog or wild animal to get a bait of fermenting beer mash at a still, get drunk, and fall in.

My guess is they never bothered to fish out the critters before cooking the mash. Once when I joined officers on a still raid, I saw a good-sized pig floating in the mash. Even with so much "road kill" added to the recipe and a good chance to go blind or die, folks just kept drinking it.

I tasted moonshine once. It was the most awful stuff I had ever put in my mouth, right up there with castor oil. Maybe they hadn't fished the pig out.

You cannot imagine the smell that emanates from one of these hooch factories. I've never been able to describe that "aroma" to my satisfaction, or anybody else's. I heard it described once as something like a cross between a beer-stained sweatshirt, cheap tequila, and a sun-ripened garbage bin. I don't know what cheap tequila smells like, or good tequila for that matter. As for the rest of it, that description pretty much nails it.

Chapter 5

Waging the Moonshine War

Even "Big Six" would've applauded the time my dad used a county school bus to search for moonshiners.

It was not a pretty world in which to wage a war. The moonshine business had a seedy underbelly that could be dangerous for lawmen. Mess with a man's livelihood and he's liable to get perturbed.

And while the danger was nowhere near the level that today's officers face in battling the drug industry, the risk was still there. Many lawmen have been killed on moonshine raids.

Retired ATF agent Steve Whitlow of Gastonia, North Carolina, a native of Lawrence County who knew my dad, can attest to that. As a young agent, he and two fellow officers raided a moonshine operation near Tuscaloosa. The moonshiner gunned down two agents, fired his gun at Whitlow, and missed. The moonshiner was killed in Whitlow's return fire.

Officers knew the danger and knew that trouble could strike at the most unexpected times. So an upcoming still raid was more than enough to get the adrenalin pumping.

And there were plenty of raids during my dad's tenure as sheriff. After the first few months in office, he and his fellow officers had axed or dynamited 117 stills and quit counting.

**At a still site: From left, Deputy Theo Rucker,
Chief Deputy Hot Rod Harris, author Jack Smith
as a teenager, and the author's father,
Sheriff Franklin Smith.**

My father said the number of "still kills" continued to increase as more and more stills were spotted and as more and more tips came in on still locations. Informants had learned that a tip would be acted on and that it would remain confidential. At times my dad and his deputies were finding so many stills they didn't have the manpower to stake out officers to catch the distillers. The lawmen would just hang a hatchet on their belts and go through the woods chopping up the illegal booze factories.

At the end of his two terms, Dad got to figuring just how many stills had been destroyed in Lawrence County during his eight years as sheriff. He came up with more than one thousand, which may have been conservative. During that time he counted more than two hundred distilling arrests and said that number may have reached three hundred.

Little wonder then that readers of the county newspaper, *The Moulton Advertiser*, were getting weekly reports of the moonshine war with stories like this on January 28, 1954:

8 Stills Busted in Busy 2 Days

The still-busting boys of Lawrence County had two field days Monday and Tuesday of this week when they smashed eight stills with a total capacity of 6,600 gallons. They took (destroyed) 4,100 gallons of mash.

Or headlines like these. . .

Sheriff Force Hits Still, Two Are Arrested at Scene
Discovery of Still, Whiskey Results in One Arrest
Three Stills, Eight Arrests Reported for Week by Sheriff
Big Still Axed at Mt. Springs
Sheriff Gets 250 Gallons of Whiskey in Late Sunday Raid

Stills were being axed and dynamited so frequently it was news when the sheriff's office had none to report. "No Stills Destroyed This Week" ran the headline in the local paper on February 17, 1955.

My father, center, and deputies Claude Lee Terry, left, and Hot Rod Harris at one of the thousand Lawrence County moonshine stills destroyed in the 1950s.

My father books another bootlegger.
Left: my mother

I gathered from my father and the deputies that no two raids were exactly the same. Expect the unexpected they said, and be patient. Most raids were preceded by perhaps hours of hiding in the bushes, enduring the cold or swatting mosquitoes, and waiting patiently for the moonshiners to show up. Once they began work, officers sprang to action, collaring whichever moonshiner was closest. Some smaller stills had one or two men workers, others had four or more.

My dad lay in the woods so much on still watches that he continually took ill from the dampness and cold.

"It seemed that he was always in the hospital with pneumonia or flu," said my sister, who, like my mother, constantly fretted over the state of his health.

But he was having fun, doing what it seemed he was born to do, and it was worth the hospital stays when a raid came off right.

Like this one . . .

On Tuesday, July 13, 1954, deputies spot a still fifteen miles southwest of Moulton in the Bankhead National Forest. At three o'clock on Thursday morning the full sheriff's force and ATU officer Clint Hamilton meet at the sheriff's office and head into the night to surround the still. Under cover of darkness, five officers settle into their places. It is 3:30 a.m.

They wait. Patience is the norm for nearly all still raids.

Three and a half hours later – good daylight now at 7 o'clock – two men make their way to the still, unaware they're being watched by The Ghost and his fellow officers. The men pour sugar into the brew – "charging" the still as officers put it. The officers pounce. The two distillers, a 20-year-old and a 30-year-old, are arrested, carried to jail, and charged with operating a distillery. The 1,350-gallon still is axed. A Jeep is confiscated, as are fuel cans, fuel oil, tubing, and 400 pounds of sugar.

It is a winter day in 1953. Another raid, this one a bit more complicated. If the plan works, the lawmen will get a still *and* a transporting arrest.

It is Monday morning, early. Sheriff's officers and state ABC agents are hunting a still they believe to be about four miles south of Moulton. They get lucky. The still is medium size, about five hundred gallons. They also discover thirty gallons of moonshine hidden nearby. Two officers hide in sight of the whiskey with portable police radios. They wait and watch. Other officers sit in a car about two miles away. They wait.

The all-day stakeout ends at 8 p.m. "He's coming for the whiskey," the officers radio the police car. A man who looks to be in his early thirties drives a '40 model Mercury near the whiskey. He loads it into the trunk and heads out of the woods to deliver his goods.

"He's on his way!"

"10-4."

The police car officers stop the whiskey-laden vehicle without incident. They confiscate the car, arrest the driver for transporting, and take him to jail.

The next day deputies Hot Rod Harris and Theo Rucker, along with ABC agents, return to smash the still.

Dad wasn't afraid to be creative either. Case in point: He had recruited Wyckoff Terry, his son-in-law, to make the raid, just the two of them watching two men work a small still near Hillsboro, a moonshine hotspot in the northern part of the county. As the two men continued to work at the still, Dad whispered to Wyckoff, "When we go in we'll go in yelling and hollering and throwing our hands in the air."

"And that's what we did," said Wyckoff. "I mean we were yelling and screaming and jumping up and down with our hands waving over our heads. We ran toward the still like wild men. The moonshiners must've gone into shock. They threw their hands in the air and started jumping around too."

I still wonder if my dad had those two men figured out, or if he was just having fun. Either way it worked. And I've been envious of Wyckoff ever since. I went on a few raids, and not one moonshiner ever showed his face. My only reward was mosquito bites and dug-in redbugs all over my body.

Except for perhaps the noisy Hillsboro raid, my father left little to chance in his drive to cut the Lawrence illegal liquor business down to size. He cultivated informants throughout the county. Hunters turned out to be a big ally. He'd ask them to watch for stills.

One hunter said: "He'd tell us if we spotted a still to just keep on walking. Pretend you don't see it because there's a good chance the moonshiners will be watching you."

Many a still was taken out through tips from hunters. We'll never know how many, of course, because my dad would never tell.

I was but a high school junior when he enlisted me to make contact with an informant. I was a little hesitant but thrilled to be involved in a real undercover job. At least I called it undercover. That sounded more dramatic when I told my friends about it. The year was 1951.

These were the days when segregation still ruled the South, and that included segregated baseball teams. Blacks played against blacks and whites played against whites, and for all we knew at that time the twain might never meet. It would be but three years before Martin Luther King Jr. was installed as pastor of Dexter Avenue Baptist Church in Montgomery and just four years before Rosa Parks, a black Montgomery seamstress, would be arrested for refusing to give up her bus seat to a white passenger.

The civil rights flame had been lit, though we didn't know it, and we certainly had no clue as to its profound consequences. One thing for sure, it had not reached the baseball game that my daddy sent me to on the outskirts of town.

All the players were black, as were nearly all the spectators, one of whom was supposed to tell me when a big load of moonshine whiskey would be hauled off the mountain. One black spectator, maybe in his thirties, had on the clothes my dad said he would be wearing. He nodded to me and I knew he was the one. I sidled up by him as nonchalantly as I knew how and, looking intently at the game, said, "Have you got the information?" He gave it to me, looking straight ahead. I killed a little more time then got in the car, let out a big sigh of relief, and carried the information to my dad.

I will admit that I don't know whether they caught that load of whiskey or whether the information was any good. But a seventeen-year-old playing out a role like they have in the movies...okay, I got carried away there. It wasn't that big of a deal. But it was worth remembering.

The small operators traditionally accused lawmen of "catching the little'uns and letting the big'uns go."

My father dispelled that notion soon after taking office. He and his deputies cornered a big'un, one of the kingpins, early on Monday morning west of Moulton. While my dad would never say, undoubtedly the arrest came from a tip by an informant or else there would have been no reason for them to be on that remote road before daylight.

The bootlegger was known to have run a family operation in and around the national forest and, it was widely believed, had staked out a gangland style territory in the mountains. To venture there, it was said, was to put your life in danger. That included other moonshiners.

On this day the kingpin was driving what was described as a "late-model car conditioned for excessive speeds." In the trunk was twenty-five gallons of moonshine. They arrested him, confiscated his souped-up car and the whiskey, and took him to jail. He was out of jail within minutes after posting a $750 appearance bond.

And when Circuit Clerk Ernest Shelton put the car up for sale at a public auction, the moonshiner had the last laugh. He bought it back.

Informants were valuable, yes. But my dad would use any technique that he felt would help him win some of the moonshine battles. He must have sat up nights figuring out how to catch a whiskey maker or bootlegger.

A map turned out to be a valuable asset. Not just any map, but a map that showed creeks in detail. Stills are along creeks. Creeks provide water. Water is needed to ferment the mash. Which is why Lanier Sibley, my first cousin, and I were sitting in Hayden Coffey's home at Wren just south of Moulton on a coldish morning in early February 2009.

We were drinking coffee and eating some of Mrs. Coffey's pecan pie, which, if she ever entered it in the county fair, would surely bring home a blue ribbon. It was so delicious we near about forgot what we came for: to talk about the map and the days when Mr. Coffey was a valued ally in the ongoing moonshine war.

"I think you ought to talk to Mr. Coffey," Lanier had said in a call a few days previously. "He knows a whole lot about Uncle Franklin."

And he did.

"Let me show you the map," he said, pulling out an 11-by-14-inch sheet with the detailed outline of the 189,000-acre Bankhead National Forest that included the 80,000-acre Black Warrior Wildlife Management Area, which lay in Lawrence and Winston counties.

"See those little red lines?" he asked. "Those are creeks. Your daddy just had to have one of those maps because the creeks would lead him to stills," said Coffey, who retired as manager of the Black Warrior Wildlife Management Area in 1984. "He was so impressed with the map that he got extra copies for his deputies. Once he started cutting stills down and arresting bootleggers out there, a lot of them went out of business or moved across the county line into Winston County."

And then he revealed another ally: church groups.

"Oh, the church people were his people," Coffey said. "They were his biggest supporters. They'd just had enough of the bootleggers. They liked to read those stories in the paper where he was cutting up stills and arresting boot-leggers. When he took office, the moonshine business was just rampant. I could give you a list of bootleggers around here at that time as long as my arm. I won't. But I could. It took him about four years to get it straightened out."

At Coffey's invitation, my father spoke at Pleasant Grove Baptist Church "two or three times." That came as a bit of a shock. I had never pictured him making speeches, and I never knew he had spoken at churches. My sister was surprised to learn that as well.

What did he talk about, I wanted to know?

Coffey grinned. "Well, the subject of bootlegging did come up."

Moreover, Coffey revealed, he spoke at several churches around the county. I did know he was a believing Christian. He was a deacon at his home church in Mt. Hope and a member of the Moulton Baptist Church during his years as sheriff.

But to see my dad speaking before a church congregation? What a thrill that would have been.

Maybe that side of him helps explain why so many of the moonshiner types he put in jail had deep respect for him. I mean the fact that he approached his job as a Christian no matter who he dealt with. Do unto others...

I know of a man in Lawrence County who was a major league player in the bootlegging business in the '50s. My daddy or his deputies arrested him many times during those eight years. He could hide whiskey where Dick Tracy couldn't find it. And while my daddy did find enough to make occasional arrests, he often left the man's place shaking his head.

"I know it was there," he would say. "I just couldn't find it."

But never was there acrimony. My daddy respected the bootlegger as a person. The bootlegger respected my dad as someone with a job to do. Nothing personal, just professional. Most of those he arrested understood that and respected him for it.

And so it was with this man.

He was in my dad's hospital room the night Dad died. The bootlegger left crying.

No longer in the business, he didn't feel comfortable talking about all that for this book. I understand. And I want him to know that Patsy and I and our families continue to respect him as our dad did and just as he respected our dad.

We will be forever touched by his caring and support on that sad night nearly a half-century ago.

I was surprised to learn that mutual respect between moonshiners and the lawmen who dogged them was not that unusual. Research for this book uncovered example after example of that.

In my journalism classroom at Auburn we studied an Associated Press feature story on the legendary "Big Six" Henderson, a federal revenuer who roamed the Kentucky hills for twenty-eight years, smashing stills and arresting moonshiners.

That man reminds me of my dad, I thought. Not that they both fought moonshining, but in how those they arrested reacted. Moonshiners even named their children after Big Six.

"I never regarded them [moonshiners] as doing anything evil, just illegal," Big Six told AP writer Jules Loh. "And I never abused them." That's exactly what my dad would have said.

As is my dad, Big Six is gone, dead at eighty-three.

He and my father would've loved knowing each other. Maybe they do.

One thing they'd talk about would be how moonshiners loved their business. It wasn't that once a moonshiner always a moonshiner, but it was true in a lot of cases. It just seemed to get in the blood.

Here's a true story of one of those men.

He looked to be in his fifties when he told of his miracle getaway with a load of moonshine whiskey. He was a Lawrence County native who had been involved in some shady dealings in his life.

For the most part, though, he'd managed to stay out of jail, at least for any extended time. His farm was mostly wooded; a creek provided fresh water. He had the perfect place to make moonshine. He came home one day to find revenuers had invaded his property, lying in wait apparently for the right time to move in.

"The place was crawling with 'em," he said, not explaining exactly how he knew. His whiskey had been run off, bottled in jugs and ready to haul away to bootleggers who would rebottle it and sell it as fuel for Saturday night shindigs.

His investment of several hundred dollars was in danger.

"So what did you do, abandon the whiskey?"

"Well, no. I prayed."

"You prayed?"

"Oh, yes. I got right down on my knees amongst those jugs of whiskey and promised the Lord that if He'd let me get out of there with that load, I'd never make or sell another drop."

The Lord must have taken him at his word. The moonshiner drove out with his load of homemade hooch and saw nary a revenuer.

"And did you keep your promise?"

"For awhile, yeah."

Even Big Six would've applauded the time my dad used a county school bus to search for moonshiners.

Where he came up with this idea, I'll never know. Yes, he must have sat up nights thinking up schemes like this.

The Monroe Stephenson family in Mt. Hope had long been friends of my father. Now they were more than that even. They were supporters and confidants, and my father didn't mind seeking their advice and counsel, political or otherwise. Like my father, you never had to wonder whether they'd be there in a pinch. They are among the families our family thinks of with appreciation when we reflect on those days so long ago.

It so happened that the son of Mr. and Mrs. Stephenson, Elwyn, was a school bus driver. A junior in high school, he'd drive his bus south up on the mountain, pick up the few students who would be riding down to school, and follow the same route each afternoon to take them home.

The key here was that he didn't pick up any students until he was well up on the mountain.

On this particular morning, the day it all started, Elwyn turned the ignition key and set off on his regular route. He glanced in the mirror that reflected the interior of the bus, as he was prone to do to keep an eye on the students. What he saw was no student. A man was standing about halfway back, balancing himself between the two rows of seats.

Startled, the youngster seemed to be trying to figure out what to do next.

"Just stay calm," my father, The Ghost, said. "I've already made this alright with your mother and daddy. Keep this to yourself. Just keep driving and I will explain."

On top of that mountain was a whiskey maker that nobody had been able to catch for years. My father was determined to put him behind bars. The moonshiner and his friends knew, or would within minutes, of every strange vehicle that drove over that lightly traveled road.

Here was the plan.

Elwyn was to drive him almost to the top of the mountain, in close proximity to where the suspected moonshiner was operating. Elwyn would slow the bus to a crawl as it reached the suspect area. My father would roll out of the moving bus and drop into a bush-covered ditch. A stopped bus with a man stepping out would have sent red flags flying. My dad would stay under cover throughout the day watching traffic and activity that might have a moonshiner feel. Elwyn would continue on, pick up his first students, come back down the mountain, and unload them at Mt. Hope School.

In the afternoon, he'd deliver the students, then start driving slowly, looking for a white ribbon tied to a bush.

He'd ease the bus door open, never stopping. My dad would jump from the bushes and onto the moving bus seemingly in one motion. Armed with binoculars, a camera, thermos bottle, and a hatchet that hung from his belt, he would spend the day scouting the area and checking the tag numbers of trucks that might be hauling sugar or cornmeal.

"It got to the point that I'd just leave the keys in the bus, and when I'd come out on a winter morning, he'd already have the bus warmed up," the younger Stephenson said. "I knew I was breaking the rules, and if I had been caught they'd have taken the bus away from me. I reckon since that was fifty years ago they can't do anything about it now. Besides, I would've done anything for that man. He was my hero."

Who won that moonshine skirmish in the early years of my father's second term? Neither. And both. My father never caught the elusive moonshiner because the moonshiner just decided to quit the business.

Stephenson and his wife, Melba, today live in retirement near Mt. Hope High School, where he was a star athlete who earned a college basketball scholarship.

He talks fondly of his association with my father.

During my dad's first term, Elwyn, as a twelve-year-old, viewed him as another Wyatt Earp. "I'd strap on my cap pistol and I'd walk downtown in Mt. Hope pretending I was Franklin Smith," he said. A few short years later he was involved in the real-life task of helping the sheriff battle the moonshiners.

"Franklin Smith was in the mold of Buford Pusser," Stephenson said, referring to the Tennessee sheriff who was the subject of the movie *Walking Tall*. "Franklin Smith was a special man."

My father did in fact walk tall for most of his eight years as sheriff, and he had a lot of success in the moonshine war. But occasionally he'd strike out or a moonshiner would outfox him.

I heard about this indirectly from a moonshiner. At the time the moonshiner saw my dad driving up the dirt road to his house, he was burying pints of whiskey in a nearby field. As was a common practice, bootleggers would hide the hooch, take the pay from a customer, and tell them where to find the planted booze, but it was always somewhere away from the house. The quick-thinking bootlegger, fearful that somebody had tipped the sheriff off to what he was doing, told his sons: "Get in the car, and as soon as he gets up here hightail it out going as fast as you can." So they did.

Just as they had hoped, my dad spun his squad car around and chased after the decoy vehicle. Of course, he found nothing illegal in the vehicle once he caught up with it. In the meantime, the bootlegger retrieved his whiskey and hid it well away from the house, just in case the sheriff came back poking around. As far as I know, he didn't.

And then there's the case of the little girl, about twelve, who would sit on whiskey like a hatching egg for her bootlegging father.

They would come to Moulton on a Saturday afternoon and ride around the square in their pickup truck looking for a customer. The little girl's job: sit on a bottle of whiskey until he could sell it.

She said in later years that her father knew the sheriff wouldn't make her get out of the truck even if he searched the vehicle. She was probably right. My father would not have embarrassed the youngster. At the time, she said, she hated my father with a passion. As an adult, she said she looks more kindly on the sheriff, adding that it might have set her father straight if he had been arrested.

And there were times when you couldn't figure if my dad was being duped or whether he planned it that way.

Like the time Johnny Mac Mecham drove into the parking area at Ray Mitchell's store a half mile or so from downtown Mt. Hope. He was astride his new motorcycle. He'd ridden it the thirty-five miles from his job in Florence, except he didn't come straight home. He had stopped in Leighton, in wet Colbert County, on the way back and filled his saddlebags with beer.

And then my father drove up.

Dang!

Johnny Mac said later all he could think about was the saddlebag beer. The word had already gotten around that the sheriff would throw you in jail for even a little bit of beer, and there he was with beer on both sides of his saddlebag.

"Johnny Mac," my father said, walking toward the motorcycle, "I've always wanted to ride on one of those things. How 'bout taking me for a little spin?"

So they rode off down toward Uncle Merrill's place, my father on the rear, his legs all but touching the beer. In a few minutes they were back.

"Whatcha got in those saddlebags, Johnny Mac?"

"Nothing, sheriff. Just some tools for my motorcycle."

My father grinned, got in his car, and left.

Then the debate started. Did the sheriff suspect that Johnny Mac had beer? Or did he just let it pass?

My take is that he knew something illegal was on that motorcycle and that it probably was beer. He could read nervousness like a fortune teller reads tea leaves. And Johnny Mac was nervous. I'm pretty sure my dad was just messing with Johnny Mac, just having fun watching him sweat. And despite what people thought, he never did get too excited about a little beer. It was moonshine that would wipe a smile off his face.

Like the encounter with Johnny Mac, my father just seemed to have the knack for being at the right place at the right time. That wasn't all luck, but some of it was.

It added to The Ghost mystique, and stories often took on a life of their own.

It got so that he could've been in Seattle and still have kept the makers and drinkers in Lawrence County jumpy.

Dalton Reed of Mt. Hope lamented that a drink of liquor got awful hard to find after my father went into office. He joined some friends one Saturday to buy a jug of Bogee's most excellent Mt. Hope homebrew.

Bogee had told them where he'd stashed it. Reed said they went over to a cornfield to retrieve the jug of brew they had paid for when somebody glimpsed a black car coming down the road. Somebody yelled, "Franklin Smith!"

Panic set in, and the entire bunch flushed like a covey of quail.

"We tore out through that cornfield knocking off ears of corn – *whomp, whomp, whomp* – and jumping three rows at a time," Reed said. "And you know what? It wasn't even Franklin Smith. It was just somebody in a black car."

Some Franklin Smith stories, like those of Big Six, were told with pride by moonshiners who'd had an experience with the sheriff they called The Ghost.

This man had one of those moments of truth. He was operating a still near Hillsboro, he said, and just as a precaution had stationed four lookouts around the work area.

"Ain't no ghost can get through that many lookouts," he remembers thinking.

He worked merrily along running off a batch when he felt a tap on the shoulder.

It was The Ghost.

Chapter 6

Life in Jail

You can call her ugly if you want, but this old girl had character.

The sheriff's family shared this three-story jail with criminals. (Photo by Lanier Sibley)

Just a big old red brick rectangular building was all she was, with a bunch of jail cells inside to house her guests. For sure, the architects didn't spend much time designing her exterior.

She got jilted a few years back, a Plain Jane relegated to her lowly status as a storage building by a smart new modern jail just outside town within hollering distance of Wal-Mart. She was left behind to stand with the old buildings of downtown.

Her aging lines are obvious now. A few cracks have developed here and there. Her paint is flaking. She has rust on her cell bars. She looks tired, like she just sat down and didn't have the energy to get up. You can call her ugly if you want, but this old girl had character. And I was fortunate enough to spend some time with her in what was another world in another time.

I remembered her as much larger than her 40-by-60-foot dimensions, maybe because she was the vibrant, bustling center of law enforcement in Lawrence County. She was the perfect fit for that role in the simpler days of the '50s.

She opened her arms to moonshiners and murderers and burglars and us, the new sheriff and his family. Her gray-tiled walls echoed the clanging of cell doors and the jingling of big bronze jail keys, but also Cora's laughter and Sill's humming her favorite Lefty Frizzel song. She embraced the exuberant little Screwdriver and his ever-present smile and the hugs of the prettiest little redheaded, freckle-faced girl who ever graced the inside of a jail. Her name was Joyce.

The old girl once welcomed Jackleg, a moonshiner; and Big Richard, a killer; and Junior when he got drunk. And she'd tease you with the heavenly aroma of Luvenia's yeast rolls baking in the oven.

She was hopping in her prime. Traffic, in and out, was seemingly nonstop. Her one phone rang constantly. Pots and pans clattered in the kitchen as cooks prepared the best jail food in Alabama for the prisoners upstairs. Her guests numbered from six on a quiet Monday to two dozen or more on those weekends when it seemed that half the county was drinking and fighting and shooting and cutting one another.

She took it all in stride. Oh, she was something alright, that old girl of the 1950s whose real name was the Lawrence County Jail.

She had three stories. We lived on the ground floor. The second floor was primarily reserved for women prisoners. The third housed male prisoners.

Step out into the little alley that ran by the front door, look right, and you would see the courthouse. Walk twenty steps or so toward the courthouse and you would find yourself on Main Street. From there you'd see the square surrounding the courthouse – three small grocery stores, V. J. Elmore's five and dime, McCulloch Furniture, Shelton and McKelvey's Pool Room, Delashaw's and King's, both department stores, two banks, barbershops, jewelry stores, drugstores. Every store location around the square was filled. Business was steady.

For a family who lived in the country all our lives we sure didn't have far to go to town.

My dad took to the jail like he belonged there, which he did. He moved easily and confidently through the jail and through his duties. It took Mom a little longer to adapt, but when she did, when she got the prisoners' food part figured out, I had never seen her happier.

As did the old log house at Mt. Hope, the jail had its limitations for family living. One bedroom for Mom and Dad and a living room/bedroom that Patsy slept in – on a rollaway bed that had to be set up each night. I slept upstairs, in whatever empty cell I could find.

"My first night at the jail was terrible!" my sister said.

"I was scared to death, and it never did get a lot better. I reckon I thought that everyone in jail was there for some horrible crime. I stayed awake until the wee hours many nights thinking I heard someone coming down the stairs. If

Daddy was out on a still raid at night or was called out for something, I would sleep with Mother until he got in. I hoped he would be busy until it was time for me to get up."

As a thirteen-year-old whose age of innocence in Mt. Hope exposed her to words no worse than "gosh" or "gee whiz" or maybe a "dad burn" when I hit my thumb with a hammer, she (and our mother) had to abide the vilest language imaginable from prisoners upstairs. They would yell out a window, cursing their luck and trying to get somebody to get them out of jail. Their oaths would echo down the jail stairs too. My dad or a deputy would stop it for awhile, but when new prisoners were brought in, it started all over again. The weekenders were the worst.

Our life in jail had its downside, but Patsy and I never lacked for visits from our friends. The jail was a magnet for our school mates, most of whom had never seen the inside of a jail.

Patsy even had a Halloween party in the jail once. "That was a lot of fun," she said. "We had it on the second floor of the jail in a big cell, and I think all the kids in town came. We decorated the cell with cornstalks and pumpkins."

Another jail perk for Patsy, and for me, was the some-times too convenient location of the City Grill.

"One of my favorite memories was going out the jail's back door through the City Grill's back door and having Mrs. Reed cook me hot French fries," she recalled.

"That and going up the street after school to Sandlin's Rexall Drug Store and letting Phil Hardy make me lemonade."

While Patsy had to forgo her own room with all her girly things and was forced to adapt to the seamier side of life at an age too young, I was more than happy. How many teenage boys get to live in the hubbub of an honest-to-goodness jail and can go and come when they please? I spent my junior and senior year in high school as a full-time resident of the jail. I went off to college, and when I came home I came home to jail. I had no room to decorate with pictures of Lou Boudreau or Ted Williams or a bed of my own or a radio beside my pillow from which I could hear the futility of the St. Louis Browns games on KMOX as I had done in Mt. Hope.

It never occurred to me to be afraid. All the prisoners were locked up, so they couldn't hurt me, at least not while I was sleeping.

I can understand Patsy's wanting a room of her own, and now that I think about it, she paid a much heavier price than I imagined being the sheriff's daughter. I didn't care whether I had a room or not. Life in jail was exciting. And one reason was a fascinating cast of characters I felt privileged to know.

Most of the so-called characters we came to know were called trusties; that is, the sheriff trusted them enough to let them out of their cells to perform chores in and around the jail. They jumped at the chance to mop floors, wash the squad cars, and even run short errands up town to pick up perhaps a box of washing powder or baking soda. The job of "trusty" was much coveted. Anything was better than languishing behind bars twenty-four hours a day.

Perhaps my favorite was Screwdriver, the youngster brought in for stealing some change from a store. He charmed us all with his infectious optimism.

Jackleg Jackson, in his mid-forties, would run a close second to Screwdriver. He'd wash the squad cars, clean up, and mop, just happy to do anything that would keep him away from his cell. He was a master at dragging his assignments out, but not so much that he appeared to be loafing.

He was a slender, tall man who'd been arrested for hauling moonshine whiskey. When he walked, he'd flop in boots that were too big, creating a distinctive shuffle. He wouldn't talk much, just "Uh'm" when you asked a question he could answer in the affirmative. A "no" answer was just a simple, quick shake of the head. No use wasting words.

He had a certain air about him that bordered on arrogance, but I think that was just an act.

"Got the cars washed, Jackleg?"

"Uh'm," he'd say, looking at you as if you had asked the stupidest question in the world. He always carried himself like he knew more than you did and that you should feel honored that he would spend time talking with you.

But I liked Jackleg. And I think he liked me. I know he had a deep respect for my father. When he thought I might have departed from the straight and narrow, he'd remind me of my obligation not to act in a way that would reflect badly on Dad.

Of course, he never claimed to be a saint himself.

"You ever do any gambling over there on deep Vine Street in Decatur?" I'd ask. He grew up in that rough and dangerous section in our neighboring town.

"Uh'm," he would answer.

"Can you set a deck of cards?"

"Uh'm."

"What about messing with dice?"

"Uh'm." His smirk told me I should've known the answer to those questions. Well, I should have. He was a cool dude with a few knife scars to prove it.

"Would you teach me to set a deck of cards?"

"Uh'm."

"And teach me how to hold the dice and how to roll them so I'll win most of the time?"

"Uh'm. But you can't tell the sheriff."

So I practiced his techniques, though of course I never put them to use. Okay, maybe a time or two in college, but I wouldn't try anything like that unless it was absolutely necessary. I learned that from Jackleg too.

The only time I ever saw Jackleg upset was once when we were outside listening to the broadcast of the famous Giants-Dodgers playoff game in October 1951. Jackleg was a big Dodger fan. Jackie Robinson was his hero. And his beloved Dodgers were just about to win the National League pennant, he thought.

When Bobby Thomson hit that now-famous "shot heard round the world" to win the pennant for the Giants, he took it hard. Mostly, he just slunk around the rest of the day and pouted.

Jackleg went off to the Kilby Prison to serve his year and a day, which, if you accounted for "good time," amounted to about nine months.

We thought we had seen the last of Jackleg.

Nope. When they released him from Kilby he headed straight back to our jail.

He just showed up at the front door one day, asking if he could stay with us for awhile until he could get a job. He was still a bit indignant that a person of his stature was forced to work like a common laborer on the prison farm. I only learned then that washing cars was a step above field work in status.

Now back at his old home, he thought maybe he could continue his trusty duties in return for food and a jail cell to sleep in.

We welcomed him home. He was one of the family. Eventually, of course, he left and we never heard from him again.

Big Richard was my protector, and I think I may have finally realized why. He was about 6-foot-3 and weighed every bit of 300 pounds. Like Jackleg, he was a trusty.

I had noticed that Big Richard stayed close to me whenever I went anywhere in or around the jail. One day I asked him why.

"Well, Mr. Jackie," he said, "they be some mean folks in this jail, and I'm not about to let any of 'em hurt you."

"No, no, Big Richard, they're not going to hurt me," I protested.

"Mr. Jackie, you don't know that. And if they as much as lift a finger to you, they going to answer to Big Richard." Unknown to me, he already had made that threat to the prisoners upstairs.

Big Richard kept an eye on me for all the time he was at the jail. Then one day he stepped on the olive green bus from Kilby Prison and went off to serve his life sentence for killing a man with a .410-gauge shotgun.

The man was his son. Big Richard was drunk.

In 1960, Richard McGuire was paroled after serving less than nine years of his sentence.

As a teen at the time, it never occurred to me that this kindly man was grieving over the loss of a son, intensified undoubtedly by the inescapable fact that he was the cause of it. In the passing years, I have often thought of Big Richard and wondered whether his obsession to keep me safe could have been tied to the loss of his own son. I'm no psychiatrist, but on reflection I think it might have been.

One man in that jail I *was* afraid of. He was a convicted murderer named Ed Mack Owen. He was gaunt, pale, and smoked a lot. He was in jail when we moved in. His appeals seemed to just go on and on until he finally went off to the state prison. He was the prisoner people asked you about when they learned you lived in the jail.

Ed Mack was sort of a celebrity. His trial generated a lot of publicity and his name seemed always to be in the paper. Other prisoners deferred to him. He tried to talk to me whenever I was on the third floor, but I kept the conversations short. He was the first murderer I had ever known.

My first face-to-face encounter with him went something like this:

"Hey, boy, you the new sheriff's son?"

"Yes, sir," I answered deferentially.

"Would you mind bringing me a pack of cigarettes? Camels. I'll pay you when my wife comes to visit."

I don't remember if I got the cigarettes or not. I probably did, but I kept my distance from Ed Mack after that.

No doubt who my sister's favorite trusty was: John Franklin Cowan.

He was of average height, maybe a bit under six feet, but he was all muscle; he had biceps like an NFL linebacker. His build was much like that of Joe Frazier, the heavyweight boxer of many years later.

John Franklin's physique could be intimidating until you got to know him. He laughed a lot and never seemed to have a bad day. His sunny disposition, despite his sentence to a jail term for a misdemeanor, made him fun to be around.

John Franklin gave you the impression that he was exactly where he wanted to be: close to a lot of good food. Which may be the reason he had a thing going with the cook, a petite little lady named Sill.

Patsy and I, and most especially my mom and dad, never viewed John Franklin as a criminal. He was more like a trusted favorite uncle. When Patsy got the itch to learn to drive, my dad and mom were so tied up with their own duties they had little time for the frustrating job of teaching a child to drive.

But John Franklin had time.

My parents never had a qualm about him taking Patsy out in one of the sheriff's squad cars and teaching her to maneuver that big vehicle around the square or down Courtland Road. Patsy trusted him implicitly. It took time *and* patience, and John Franklin had both. I imagine plenty of folks around Moulton in those days of the '50s did a double-take when they saw this pretty young white girl chauffeuring a big black man who could pass for a heavy-weight boxer.

"Myrtle, if you're standing up, sit down. You're not going to believe what I saw in town this morning."

"He was a precious person who would have fought for me," Patsy said of her mentor. "Mother and Daddy trusted him with my life."

Since I could type and had a portable typewriter, my dad would often ask me to come up to a cell to take down a confession. The prisoner would confess. I would take it down word for word, or as close as I could come, while my dad prodded the prisoner and helped him think of the right words. Then the prisoner would sign it, and I was done.

At least that's what I thought until one day I was subpoenaed to testify in court about a confession I had typed. The defense attorney questioned my motives, my skill at typing, my intelligence, my honesty, and just about anything else he could think of. I sweated. I grew up a little each time I sat in that witness chair and I think Dad sort of enjoyed seeing me learn to handle tough questions. Once I learned what to expect, I rather enjoyed testifying in court.

I loved the courtroom, especially when Circuit Solicitor George Johnson was over from Athens to prosecute a felony case. George Johnson was the most flamboyant prosecutor I had ever seen at work. He was a little slumped and wore loose-fitting dark suits and a tie that hung a good six inches below his belt buckle.

With his turn to cross-examine a defense witness, he'd rise slowly from his seat and glare at his prey, who he apparently felt obligated to destroy. But not right at the moment. He'd lob a few softball questions. Then about the time the defendant had begun to relax from the glare,

Johnson would fire tough questions one after the other, his voice one of scorn. I've seen many a defense witness wilt under his heat, become confused, stumble for answers. About the time the witness had formulated an answer, Johnson would turn his back on the witness, face the jury with an air of disgust, and say, "No more questions," as if the witness was too contemptible to even bother with.

Those tactics are common in the courtroom, but George Johnson had mastered every nuance.

Oh, and those closing arguments! I would have bought a ticket to watch his performance, and a performance was what it was. He'd start calmly in a soft voice and pick up speed and volume. Shortly, he'd be exhorting the jury to remove this evil man from society. A jury went along with him more often than not. He sent a lot of evil men from Lawrence County to the pen.

George Johnson was who I wanted to be.

I was a big sports fan at that stage of my life. I never tried to talk my dad out of jailing anybody except on two occasions.

"Dad, do you know who that is?" I asked when he brought in a hefty young man one night. He'd been on a drinking spree and somebody called the law.

"No, but what difference does it make?" was his answer or something close to it.

"He's an All-American end," I said. "Couldn't you just let him go?"

I knew what the answer would be, but somehow I felt embarrassed. My football heroes weren't supposed to find themselves in jail. He was soon free on bond and back on the football field at a Southeastern Conference school that fall.

The other time was when a pitcher in the Boston Red Sox organization was brought in, again for a relatively minor offense. Same request for leniency. Same answer.

On that occasion I did engage in a conversation with the baseball player. I think he started it, just to let us know that he was a big-time athlete. I hinted that I was not in agreement with my dad. He pitched for a minor league Triple-A team, he told me, and was hoping to make it to the big leagues. I tried to keep up with his career after that, but I never recall hearing of him again.

Stars didn't impress my dad, and I guess I would have been disappointed if they had.

My dad and mom ran the jail informally but not too informally. They let Screwdriver have the run of the place, but at his young age his situation was different. The jail did have a Mayberry feel to it though. I can see how this real-life scene could well fit the Mayberry format. Think of my mother in this case as Aunt Bee.

My mother was helping the cook prepare lunch for the prisoners when she looked up to see a young man standing in the kitchen door.

"Mrs. Smith, you can tell Mr. Franklin that if he wants me I'm going over to the hospital to get something for my nervousness," he said politely.

She didn't recognize that he was a prisoner until he offhandedly remarked that he had "locked that man up." "That man" turned out to be John Coleman, a trusty who had gone into the young man's cell to clean the floor.

As always, my mother kept her cool. She promised that she would see that he got his medicine and calmly led him back upstairs to his cell. By that time, Coleman's shouts for help were echoing down the tiled walls.

She released the trusty, descended the stairs, and I'm sure she and the cook had a big laugh. Just another moment of innocence and trust in the Lawrence County Jail.

I don't rightly list our cooks as "characters," but they sure were folks who made life interesting around the jail.

Consider Sill Bankston: thin, trim, neat, believed in Jesus but would take a drink for medicinal purposes, off-duty of course. At work she hummed a lot and laughed a lot and generally made life happier on the first floor. She was a good cook too. Her trusty sweetheart, John Franklin, sure thought so.

She hummed mostly Lefty Frizzell songs. "If You've Got the Money, Honey, I've Got the Time" was her favorite. "That Lesty Cazell sure can sing," she would say.

I don't know how we found Sill. Maybe she was just looking for a job and we got lucky.

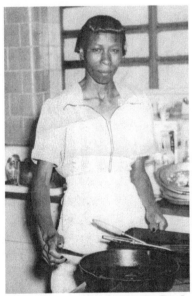

Sill Bankston cooked and hummed a happy tune.

How Maude Addison got a job as a cook turned out to be one of the more heartwarming stories of my dad's two terms in office.

Maude's fifteen-year-old son, Adam, was in jail for a relatively minor non-violent offense. The family couldn't muster the few hundred dollars for an appearance bond that would have released him. Maude lived five miles outside Moulton. She visited her son every day. She had no transportation. So sometimes she walked to the jail, and sometimes she caught a ride. Didn't matter. She was determined to check on her son.

We looked forward to her visits too. She was down-to-earth, soft-spoken, and you could just tell she was a good woman.

My mother thought so, and my mother was a good judge of character, though in this case I think sympathy was her prime motivator.

So with the jail in need of a cook, my mom and dad talked it over. See if Maude could cook. She could. Offer her the job and a place to stay. A woman shouldn't be hitchhiking or walking on a public road. The place to stay was an empty cell on the women's floor. She was only too happy to accept. That solved the transportation problem.

Oh, and would she mind if they assigned Adam to be her assistant in the kitchen?

I don't recall my mom or dad describing Maude's reaction. But I sure wish I'd been there to see it.

Talk about two happy people. (Put Mom and Dad on that list too.) Maude and her son would talk and laugh. Life was good again. I don't know how much Adam helped his mother. But he sure could play the guitar. The kitchen never sounded so good.

And then there was Luvenia Taylor, our first cook. She set the standard by which all the other cooks were measured.

She was a tall woman who carried herself with assurance. She came to us with the reputation as the best cook in Moulton. She was, undoubtedly. Everything she prepared was five-star good, but her yeast rolls were just too good for this world. Walk in the front door of the jail and smell that aroma and you knew you were in for a special treat.

The matrons of Moulton, when they were having a dinner party, would ask Luvenia if she could spare the time to make yeast rolls for their guests. She did that a lot.

Luvenia was pleasant and easygoing, but you didn't mess around in her kitchen. She was a clean fanatic, and everything had to be just so. She'd carry a little dip of snuff in her lower lip though. And if you riled her, she'd turn those stony brown eyes toward you and pooch that already low lip out at you. She didn't have to say a word; you knew to straighten up or get gone.

"Luvenia was the disciplinarian," Patsy said. "She would fuss on me in a minute if I was acting in a way that she didn't approve. But I loved her dearly."

So you figured Luvenia cooked those heavenly yeast rolls just for our family? No, sir. Whenever we had yeast rolls, the prisoners had yeast rolls. In fact, we ate the same food the prisoners did, whatever it was.

Cora Locklayer I never knew. She was the cook while I was in college. Patsy just thought the world of her.

She too was a pleasant woman, laughed a lot, knew how to cook, and became especially close to our family.

When Patsy and Wyckoff were married in 1957 at Moulton Baptist Church, Cora was right there in her Sunday best sitting on the back pew, a lone black woman among a sanctuary filled with whites, this in a time of rigid segregation. Even now, Patsy says she can feel again the warmth and love she felt for Cora at the instant she spied her seated in the back of the church waiting to see her "child" take her wedding vows.

Cora Locklayer watched her "child" get married.

Back at the jail Cora took her place as a blue-ribbon cook.

"All my friends loved to come to the jail and eat," Patsy said. "They thought I was so lucky to be in a position to have cooks *and* be petted to death by them. Plus the food was delicious."

It would be hard to overstate how good the food was. Patsy remembers it this way:

Food was wonderful with all four cooks. Luvenia's yeast rolls were the envy of everyone. The prisoners always had a great breakfast – scrambled eggs, grits, fried "fat back" or bacon or sausage, and sometimes fried bologna. They always had homemade buttered biscuits and King

Bee syrup. The breakfast drink was either milk or coffee. Sometimes a small carton of orange juice was put on the tray.

Lunch was fresh vegetables when in season, a meat – many times it was meatloaf, fried chicken, or ham. If the vegetables were canned, all the cooks "doctored" them up until they were delicious. The prisoners always had a dessert with lunch, usually a sheet cake with icing or a carton of ice cream. Sill made blackberry cobbler or some kind of fruit pudding. Luvenia was known to make the best banana pudding in town, so the prisoners always looked forward to that. And the meal was topped off with those homemade rolls! When the cooks other than Luvenia were there the prisoners had bought rolls or hot cornbread. The drink was usually iced tea.

J. C. Taylor was Luvenia's husband. He worked as a janitor at the courthouse and would usually come across the street to the jail and eat lunch with Luvenia after the prisoners were fed.

Supper was the same as lunch if we had enough leftovers. If not, the prisoners got soup and two sandwiches and a dessert or a piece of fruit. They sure didn't go hungry.

The metal plates the food was served on were put on a huge tray and sent upstairs on a small elevator called a "dumbwaiter." A deputy or trusty would meet it upstairs and distribute plates to the prisoners through a small slot in the jail doors.

As tasty as the food was, the prisoners were not beyond complaining.

My lifelong friend, Bobby Terry, remembers visiting the jail when, as high school classmates, we went upstairs at lunchtime. The prisoners were already eating, he recalled, and said I asked them if they had asked God to bless their food.

They said they had, Bobby remembered. But they would be happy to recite it again. And they did.

"God above us, look down upon us,

"And bless this tainted ham.

"Give us something better to eat,

"'Cause this fatback ain't worth a d---!'"

Which was followed by knee-slapping laughter.

Of all the nerve! They should've been put on bread and water.

That refrain, I learned later, was something of a standard for prisoners, including ours, even when they were eating banana pudding or Luvenia's yeast rolls.

But that's all in the past now, just another fading memory for a red brick building that took on a personality of her own.

Fifty years later, the old lady, once young and vibrant and exciting, is a lonely creature filled with somber silence and stored boxes. Her trusties, her cooks, her good-people-gone-bad boarders, her sheriff's family – they're all gone now. The sheriff and his wife are deceased. So are most others she protected during her first time to host a county sheriff.

But sometimes when the moon is bright and shadowy creatures are astir, if you listen with your heart, those old walls still echo with Cora's laughter, the strains of Adam's guitar, the rattle of the keys, and the clanging of cell doors. Listen with your heart and you will hear Sill humming softly another of her "Lesty Cazell" tunes, my dad's voice recalling the events of the day, my mom praying for us all.

That great old girl we called the county jail can hear them now, late at night, just as can those of us whose lives she changed, when the wind whistles down the alley and memories come out of hiding.

Lawrence Sheriff Gene Mitchell leads my father's four great granddaughters through the old jail that was also the sheriff's home in the 1950s. From left, Mitchell, Reagan Cunningham, Claire Smith, Ruby Cunningham and Maggie Smith. (Photo by Suzanne Terry Cunningham)

Chapter 7

The '54 Election – Thumbs Up

This night had validated every career decision he had made . . .

When my father opened his campaign for re-election in March of 1954, our hopes were high. At that point he was arguably the most popular political figure in the county.

He was riding a wave of popularity. His moonshine war rolled on. There were no county scientific political polls in those days. But you felt it. My dad did too. He was confident, but not too confident. He was preparing for a tough race just in case he and his supporters were misreading the political winds. It had happened before.

The surprising number of opponents – five – gave him pause. That portended a runoff even if he were the top vote-getter in the primary. Garnering more than 50 percent of the vote in a field of six was unlikely.

We believed at the time that Eddie Mitchell, a popular Moulton barber with some law enforcement experience, would prove to be the strongest opponent. Two former sheriffs, J. Kumpe Ayers and G. D. Byars, had entered the race. A colorful Courtland officer with years of experience was running. He was W. L. "Son" Terry, and people were wondering if old "Son" had too much personality to be a serious contender.

And then the candidate who was even harder to handicap: Clarence "Hot Rod" Harris, the former chief deputy and now police chief of Courtland. He had name recognition, experience, and a tough-on-criminals reputation.

Still, it was Eddie Mitchell who we thought posed the biggest threat. We didn't think it would happen, but if he did win, the county would have a good man as sheriff. Mitchell had been a civic leader in Moulton and knew a lot of people.

Another unknown in that race was whether the moonshine industry would or could throw enough money into the race to force my father out of office. In hindsight, probably not. They would wait until my father was more vulnerable and go after him in a feeding frenzy – and that's exactly what happened.

The more pressing concern at the moment, however, was those maddening political rallies. By now my dad had experience in that part of politics. But he still didn't like them.

Mt. Hope PTA scheduled a barbecue supper. A chicken plate dinner was planned for Chalybeate Junior High School. And on it went at Town Creek, Mt. Moriah, Courtland, and Plainview. Those included only the early dates. Others would be added.

The Democratic primary was to be conducted May 4. In those days, the county didn't have enough Republicans to fill a small room, much less enough to hold a primary. If you won the Democratic primary or the runoff, you won. There were no local races in the fall election. A win in May meant you had to wait until the following January to start your term.

Election night has always been a pretty big to-do in Lawrence County. This one had something extra. On this May 4, 1954, night the Moulton Volunteer Fire Department sponsored what they called an election party on the south side of the courthouse square. The firemen set up a big board on which to record the returns as they came in. A loudspeaker announced returns from various parts of the county.

I have tried to think of something comparable to election night in Lawrence in those days. The best I can come up with is that it's something like a mini Mardi Gras. Folks were in a celebrating mood, especially the winners, or they were downcast if their candidate lost. It wasn't uncommon to celebrate a win – or soothe the ache of a loss – with a nip or two of corn squeezin's. The police tended to look the other way. You could get away with more on election night than you could at any other time. Maybe not, but it sure seemed that way.

My dad was not about to start arresting folks at that party lest they had voted for him earlier in the day. It just would not have been the decent thing to do. He opened up his office in the courthouse. His supporters had a place to talk and ponder the returns until the race was decided.

He had a commanding lead before good dark. At worst he would go into a runoff.

The loudspeaker rang out the results, and the more it blared the better my father looked. He carried 29 of the county's 33 boxes, and the vote totals were even more impressive. The first unofficial count gave him 3,385 votes compared with 1,273 for runner-up Eddie Mitchell. That meant he came within 44 votes of winning without a runoff when taking into account votes for other candidates.

Ayers had 907 votes; Byars, 658; Terry, 455; and Harris, 136.

Hot Rod's vote was stunning, at least for me. That election ended his hopes for becoming sheriff of Lawrence County. He would never again be considered a serious contender for the office he coveted.

My father, as usual, kept an eye on the boxes from Mt. Hope. His friends, neighbors, and kinfolks gave him 420 votes to 215 for Mitchell, the next highest.

The official vote count brought more good news. He now lacked just 19 votes to avoid a runoff.

Mitchell bowed out of the race with this statement:

"Franklin turned in such a large vote – almost a majority in the primary – that I thought it would be best and proper to let him have it without a run-off."

Election results on this night gave him the stamp of approval he so desperately sought. He had passed the test. Yes, he had won his first race four years previously. But this was different. This night validated every career decision he had made up to this point. Looking back on my father's career from fifty years away, I am convinced that this election night was the height of his career. Never again was he to feel the overwhelming adoration and appreciation of the people he served; never again was he to feel the sense of accomplishment and satisfaction of knowing that he was not just the sheriff but a good one. The people said so.

Knowing that now but not then, the night of May 4, 1954, evokes bittersweet memories. I had never been prouder of my dad. His happiness that night was my happiness, and Patsy's and Mother's. The joy we felt that night was soon to evaporate, however.

Within two years of that spirit-lifting election night, his world – and ours with it – would be turned upside down.

Chapter 8

The Bull Escapes

Two-bit county jails held no fear for him.

It had been a long drive from Dallas. My father and I were within an hour of home.

He wanted to stop for lunch in Hamilton, Alabama; I had hoped he wouldn't do that. Every time we went into a restaurant the waitresses would stare and whisper to each other. And the diners would turn their heads and stare.

That was because we had with us Leland Herschel Bull in handcuffs and leg irons. He had escaped from the Lawrence County Jail two weeks earlier, was finally caught near Dallas, and my father and I were bringing him back to Alabama.

The waitresses on this August day whispered and stole glances at our table and set our orders down quickly and moved away in haste, all the time watching Bull trying to eat with one hand. The other hand was handcuffed to the table leg. My father went about his meal seemingly oblivious to the stir we had caused. He talked to the twenty-two-year-old escapee as though they were old friends. I think my dad enjoyed the scene. I was eighteen at the time and slightly embarrassed.

The Bull episode was among the more memorable of my father's first term as sheriff.

It had started on Tuesday afternoon, August 12, 1952, when a drab olive green bus with barred windows from Kilby Prison in Montgomery deposited a prisoner at the Lawrence County Jail. Off stepped an obviously young man in brown prison clothes, slightly built with jet black hair, standing 5 feet 4 inches high.

Bull had been returned to the county for trial on an arson charge. He had stolen a car near Birmingham in Jefferson County a year earlier and drove it into Lawrence County. Officers spotted the stolen car and gave chase. Just before he got out of Lawrence County, he set fire to the car and fled.

He was not so lucky in Jefferson County. He was arrested for the theft of that car, convicted of grand larceny, and sent to Kilby Prison. Now he was back in the jail at Moulton to stand trial for burning the car.

He stepped from the prison bus with just a hint of a swagger, enough to let you know that two-bit county jails held no fear for him. I was taken aback by a boyish appearance that seemed incompatible with his piercing dark brown eyes and smirky half-smile that seemed to say, "I'm a bad dude. So don't mess with me."

That dude made me nervous from the time he alit from the bus.

He was to be tried on that Tuesday, but the prison bus had gotten there too late. So he'd just stay in the county jail until the courts decided when to put him on trial.

"Could I have a separate cell?" he asked my father. Bull wanted no part of the bullpen where the drunks and petty violators were held.

My father agreed to his request, a decision that within hours he would wish he could take back. The main door to Bull's cellblock was locked tight. But the door to his small cell inside that block remained unlocked, giving him freedom to go outside the smaller cell and reach the outside wall.

The hacksaw blade sewn into his belt-lining had gone undetected. He had gotten it at Kilby and brought it to Lawrence County. A deputy searched him but found nothing. The pat-down may have been cursory. After all, he'd come directly from the big state prison, and if they hadn't caught it why should the deputy?

Bull said later the idea of escape just struck him as he lay on his bunk bed. Given his request for the separate cell and his hacksaw contraband, you had to know he came to Lawrence County with escape on his mind.

It was about two o'clock in the afternoon, only minutes after he had gotten off the prison bus, that he decided to put his hacksaw to use.

"I was just lying there on my bunk looking out when I saw that window and decided to get out," he later told Al Funderburke of *The Decatur Daily*.

For most of the afternoon, Bull sawed at the case-hardened steel bars on the window of his cell with little success. The job was going to take a while. He whistled as he worked to cover the sound of the hacksaw. He continually peeked through the window to see if he had been detected.

"Hey, down there, you got a cigarette?" he called several times to people passing in the alley below.

They'd peer up and move on. They never noticed his sawing. He took that as a sign he could continue without fear of detection from below.

He took a break for supper. He was lying on his bunk when the trusty brought his food. The trusty noticed nothing out of the ordinary.

After supper, he was ready to work in earnest. Eventually the bar began to give way, and just after midnight, success.

He pulled the broken bar aside, creating an opening big enough to squeeze his body through. The plan was working. For an escape rope, he tore mattress covers in his cell bunk into strips and tied them together.

But would the strips support his 145-pound body for the three-story drop? He tied them to a bar in his cell and yanked hard. He deemed them strong enough.

He tied his makeshift rope securely to a center bar on the window he had just broken and, while the little town of Moulton was asleep, squeezed his small frame through the window and slid down the homemade rope to freedom.

The time, he figured, was 12:40 a.m.

It was then, if you were to believe him, that he had second thoughts about what he'd done. After he had taken a few steps toward the back of the jail, maybe twenty feet from where I was sleeping, he was tempted to wake the sheriff and ask for forgiveness.

Nah. Just keep moving.

And he did.

At that point he was headed east and then abruptly turned in the opposite direction. He told reporter Funderburke that he circled the town, met a man, and bummed a cigarette.

He saw a City of Moulton police car rolling slowly down Highway 24 headed west, looking for him, he thought. He rolled into a ditch and then made his way through swamps and bushes around Moulton for several hours. He was back out to the highway now and saw an approaching bread delivery truck.

He thumbed the bread truck for a ride and got it, to Russellville, twenty-eight miles to the west. He helped load another bread truck in Russellville in return for a ride to Bear Creek, where his grandfather lived.

Back at Moulton, a hairdresser for a beauty shop whose back door was but a few feet from the jail came to work early that morning. She saw the mattress-cover strips fluttering in the breeze from an approaching rainstorm. She went banging on the jail door to alert the sheriff.

Neighboring sheriffs' forces, the Alabama Highway Patrol, and Moulton police were scouring the area for any signs of the escapee. Sirens wailed as officers scattered in response to early reports of escapee sightings. All were false.

A few miles to the east – nowhere close to where Bull actually was – came a report that the escapee had been seen crossing the Moulton-Decatur road.

My father, who had bought a bloodhound for the sheriff's office, wanted badly to put his new weapon to work. It was not to be on this day, because Wednesday, August 13, was the day that a severe drought was broken. Rain came down in sheets.

As it turned out, lawmen were closer to Bull than they thought. They had traced him to Bear Creek but lost his trail there.

That was probably because Bull decided not to see his grandfather. He knew the elderly man would try to convince him to turn himself in. He rambled about west Alabama near his hometown of Winfield.

With $5 he got from a bootlegger he headed toward Texas. He said he knew lawmen would be looking for him in his home territory.

He got to Dallas on Friday, hitching rides and scratching for food wherever he could find it. And he was so sleep-deprived, he said, he was making foolish decisions – including the one in which he decided to steal a car with a group of men fifteen feet away. He grabbed a rock, smashed a window, hotwired the ignition, and took off across Texas. He made it back to Dallas, stole two tags to put on the car to keep it from being identified as stolen, and headed out again.

It was in Uvalde, Texas, that his escape unraveled.

He had failed to tighten the front tag. A patrolman noticed that it was missing, pulled him over, asked for a driver's license (which he didn't have), and checked to see if the tags and car were stolen.

Affirmative, responded the radio dispatcher back in Dallas. Further checks disclosed that he fit the description of an escapee from Alabama.

His time had run out.

He admitted not only that he was the escapee but recounted in detail his every move from the time he entered the jail at Moulton six days earlier.

Bull said he picked the Texas officer to confess to "because he was a nice guy. I wouldn't talk to the others because they were too smart. But this guy was alright, so I told him."

Next stop for Bull was the Dallas County Jail. The "we-got-your-man" call came in shortly thereafter to my father. Dallas County was willing to drop the stolen car charge so he could be returned to Alabama.

"You want to go to Dallas with me?" my dad asked me.

"Texas?"

"What do you mean, Texas? Of course, Texas."

So we piled in that big old black '52 Ford heavy-duty squad car and headed out to Dallas, the tall radio antenna on the back bending in the wind. It was an exciting trip for me, not just because my father drove too fast, which he always did, but because I had never been west of the Mississippi River.

We got to Dallas on a Sunday, stayed in a mom-and-pop motel, and went to a minor league baseball game Sunday night at which Vic Damone sang "On the Street Where You Live." We picked up our prisoner the next day.

When we walked into the Dallas County sheriff's office Monday morning, you'd have thought we were representing the governor of our state. The noted Sheriff Bill Decker himself – he would become a familiar face on television following the Kennedy assassination – gave us the red carpet treatment as we toured his massive jail and sheriff's offices. I was impressed that he treated my dad as an equal.

We made it back to Greenwood, Mississippi, the first night. We dropped Bull by the local jail for the night and for once could eat without calling attention to ourselves.

My hope was that we'd make it all the way back to Moulton in time for lunch. If nothing else, we could eat at Slim Hambrick's City Grill.

Slim would want to know all about the trip anyway. We'd have fun telling about it, and he had the juiciest hamburgers in town.

But no, I had to feel embarrassed one more time as diners and waitresses stared at us in uncomfortable silence.

Back at the jail, Bull was only too happy to tell of his exploits.

He posed for a picture in front of the still unrepaired window that he escaped through and quipped, "Well, I'm right back where I started from." He never lost that little smirky half-smile. He had it all the way from Dallas, and it drove me nuts.

Leland Bull proudly poses by the third-floor jail window through which he hacksawed his way to freedom. (Microfilm image from the archives of *The Decatur Daily*)

Leland Herschel Bull was a part of life at the jail but for a short time. But his time with us and his time away from us for those memorable two weeks in 1952 created images that are fresh a half-century later.

Chapter 9

The Lighter Side of Jail Life

Now, the electrified mulberry bench wasn't all my idea.

I fear that what I am about to tell you will give you the wrong impression of my dad's two terms as sheriff of Lawrence County, Alabama. It was most assuredly not all fun and games.

People were brought through the jail doors charged with murder and assault and just about every other major crime you could think of. We watched people's lives ruined by senseless acts. We saw inherently evil people.

This was serious business, and we all, our family, the deputies, and especially my dad, treated it as such. Sometimes we had to laugh to keep from crying, and sometimes we laughed just to release the tension.

Theo Rucker was always a favorite of mine. He enjoyed being a deputy. He always brought his optimism to work.

On this rainy day you would find Theo huddled behind bushes watching a five-gallon jug of moonshine whiskey in the mountain range just south of Moulton. Other deputies had carried him to the area of the jug and then gone to their regular duties. The idea was that the owner would come to pick up the jug, at which time Theo would step into view and arrest the perpetrator. As the dreary day dragged on, nobody showed.

My dad decided the stakeout was futile, and as he and Chief Deputy Hot Rod Harris were en route to pick up Theo, my dad's mischievous mind hatched another plot.

That's how it came about that Hot Rod snuck in, grabbed the jug, and took off running.

"Halt!" yelled Theo, entering the chase with his pistol waving in the air. He finally outran his suspect and learned of the charade only when he looked into the face of his fellow deputy.

He was a good sport about it all, but it was several days before his co-workers let him forget it.

Another little episode also involved Theo. My dad never knew about it. Neither did Theo. I've been mum all these years.

You must understand that once I became a teenager and had outgrown my squeaky voice, I sounded exactly, and I mean exactly, like my father on the telephone. Everybody said so. My friends could not tell whether they were talking to me or my father. I had fun with that. About the time they'd get through telling me what they thought of that new girl in class, I would become the sheriff and they'd stammer off the line.

More than once I took calls in the sheriff's office and some disturbed citizen recognized my voice as the sheriff and just rattled off his problem before I could stop him. In those cases, I just decided to "be" the sheriff and assure the caller that we'd take care of it. Yes, I would always tell my dad.

I had been assigned to travel with Theo to the insane asylum in Tuscaloosa. I was eighteen at the time. We were to transport, as the law provided, a mentally disturbed man who had been committed by his family. It was a horrible situation. He fought and screamed and finally was restrained by a straitjacket. I felt sorry for that family, and for him.

Theo drove and I sat in the backseat with the man in the straitjacket, just to make sure he stayed calm. He did, fortunately. And by the time we were a few miles south of Moulton he didn't pose a problem.

That's when I spotted the walkie-talkie in the back floorboard. It had the same frequency as the squad cars. We were in 42-A. The other car was 42-B.

"42-B to 42-A," I said into the walkie-talkie, covering the microphone with my hands.

Theo grabbed the radio mike.

"Go ahead, sheriff."

"What's your 10-20?" I asked and then dropped the walkie-talkie in my lap. He looked out the window, surveyed the landscape, and told the "sheriff" we were ten miles south of Moulton. I glanced to see our passenger with a quizzical look on his face.

"Everything okay?" the "sheriff" asked.

He turned to me in the backseat. I dropped the walkie-talkie.

"Everything alright, Jackie?"

"Just fine," I said, smiling reassuringly at our passenger in the straitjacket.

"Everything's just fine, sheriff."

Now at this point I was getting worried. It had gone on long enough that it would be embarrassing if Theo discovered my mischief. But more importantly, I noticed our passenger had a wild look in his eyes again. He would look at Theo when he was talking, and he would turn to look at me when I was talking. Back and forth he went, the look in his eyes becoming scary, as if he were trying to make some sense of it all. He may have been trying to figure out in his own mind if he was *that* crazy. I hope I didn't add to that poor man's problems.

And then there was the beer episode.

Lawrence was, and is, a dry county. That includes beer. My dad didn't get too worked up about a can of beer. But what about a whole truckload? One will be coming through Town Creek on its way to Decatur on Highway 20, the tipster said.

He was right. There were three hundred cases on that truck. But now that you've confiscated that much brew, what do you do with it? Well, you put it in jail, of course. My dad had his haul stacked in an empty cell next to the bullpen but out of reach for a cell full of prisoners who would've given just about anything for one of those Budweisers.

I wondered if my dad didn't put it there just to mess with their minds.

If so, his ploy backfired. One of them came up with a clothes hanger, straightened it, bent one end to the approximate size of a bottle top, and went fishing.

By the time the jailer discovered just how ingenious prisoners can be, the whole bunch was as happy as happy could be. My dad confiscated the coat hanger and moved the beer, which I thought was a mean thing to do.

Now, the electrified mulberry bench wasn't all my idea. My dad can share some of the guilt.

The mulberry bench, as it came to be called, was connected on one end to the back of a store that faced the town square. The other end was attached to a mulberry tree, which provided shade to those who chose to sit there.

A lot of the older men in town did. That was because you could sit eighteen feet from the front door of the jail and see everything and everybody that went through that door. It was the best show in town, and free too.

The Mulberry Bench in the 1950s was usually occupied by the elderly men of Moulton who sat and gossiped and whittled while they watched everything and everybody that went through the jail's front door. This replica, built by Wyckoff Terry, sits in the exact location of the original bench – on private property just eighteen feet from the jail door. It was connected to a building on one end and to a mulberry tree on the other. (Photo by Lanier Sibley)

My dad became mildly irritated by the gawking. I told him I could solve his problem. He asked how. I told him. He said, "Do it."

I put two small metal strips on the bench and connected them with a wire, which I slid into a water hose.

When the bench filled up and if Dad was around, he would say, "Jackie, I believe that car needs a little water," pointing to a nearby squad car. I would pull the car close to the bench and put "water" in the car. What I did was leave the car running, put the hose under the open hood, pull a sparkplug cover, and hold the protruding wire so that the spark would jump through the hose and down the bench.

It didn't provide a big shock, just enough to be uncomfortable but not enough that the sitters would know why. The first time, our contraption worked beautifully.

One old fellow would feel the sensation and, not knowing what it was, would stand up slowly so as not to admit to being stung, brush the seat of his pants, and allow that he'd best be running along. Others followed suit.

My dad could hardly contain his laughter. We shut down the operation when an Alabama Highway Patrolman sat on the bench, got shocked, and got mad. I of course got the blame.

At the time my mother was unaware of the electrified bench.

About five years before her death my mother recalled from her nursing home bed that a highway patrolman had sat on some kind of bench that shocked him and was very upset about it.

"I've always wondered who was responsible for that," she said.

She found her answer in my guilty face.

"Jackie, you didn't!"

I was most emphatically not the cause of Peg Brown's mishap.

Peg was so named because he had a peg leg, his natural leg shot off, the rumor was, in some kind of accident. Peg was a trusty, a nervous type who always looked as though he was afraid something or someone was sneaking up behind him. He was one of the many characters who came through our jail. I doubt that Peg had ever been across the state line or further than the second grade.

But he was pretty good at mopping floors. On this day in the mid-'50s, he had mopped the kitchen and other areas in the bottom-floor living quarters except for my parents' bedroom. He had just rolled his big mop bucket into the bedroom when shots rang out.

Peg, frightened, went spread-eagled on the floor, over-turning his mop bucket and generally making a mess of things. The shots were coming from a TV set in the bedroom. Peg had never seen a TV.

He made bond not long after that. I wonder whatever happened to Peg.

Except for Peg, the most nervous prisoner I recall was Willie B. Williams. Willie B. made homebrew. The problem was he drank too much of it, got drunk, drove to town, and ended up in jail on charges of driving while intoxicated or, if he had managed to get out of his car, public drunkenness. Willie B. was our guest on a fairly regular basis.

The first time they brought him in he was being booked when he heard a cat meow. In a flash he was near the ceiling, clinging to metal bars for dear life.

"What's the problem, Willie B.?" they wanted to know as they pried his hands loose. They learned quickly enough that he panicked at the sound of a cat.

My dad made a new rule: Don't get catty around Willie B. The word of his cat phobia got around though, and there seemed to be at least one prisoner who knew how to get Willie's goat. Just say "meow!" and get ready for action.

Sound echoed down the stairwell.

"Meow!" you would hear from upstairs. You knew then Willie B. was clinging to cell bars somewhere up there, and you knew he was as high off the floor as he could climb.

I hope the statute of limitations has expired on this incident. I accept all the blame and my only excuse is that I was young, and I guess I could always use Flip Wilson's famous excuse: "The devil made me do it."

I knew there were firecrackers in the evidence room. Big old red illegal firecrackers that deputies had confiscated. I knew two other things: a thunderstorm was brewing and three deputies were in the little deputy's office just across the alley. The alley between the jail and where they were on the first floor was maybe ten feet wide. Now, if I went to the third floor of our jail, lit one of those firecrackers, and dropped it just in front of their door, why I bet that thing would make some kind of noise, just like lightning striking.

Don't get ahead of me here.

The first one worked so well I had lightning to strike three more times. *Boom!* The sound would jar that alley. *Boom! Boom!*

Here's what I learned later was going on in that room.

The three deputies did indeed think lightning was striking just outside their door. They were pretty sure they were going to die. They all – the three of them – piled atop one another on a little cot.

When it was all over we had to send a trusty with a mop bucket to clean the floor.

If those three deputies ever learned what really happened I never heard about it. When my dad came in, they told him of this terrible lightning storm that nearly killed them and how they all jumped on the cot. My dad, a little surprised, said the weather wasn't all that bad where he was.

My dad told me what they said. I eventually told him of my evil deed. I thought I heard a chuckle as he walked away.

My sister Patsy and I always got along pretty well. Except for the time she tried to kill me.

We still tease each other as big brothers and little sisters often do. After all, she is still my little sister even with the passing of a half-century. She just learned of all that stuff you've just read.

"And I thought you were sooo perfect," she said.

Well, that's what little sisters are supposed to think about big brothers.

Then she admitted her own dirty deed.

"You and I were standing in front of the jail, and as usual you were aggravating me, and I picked up a rock and threw it at you, really hoping to hit you. Well, it hit one of the windows beside the front door of the jail and broke the glass. The glass was probably bulletproof with wire in the double glass. My mother was so upset with me. She said, 'You could've killed him!' I told her that at the time that was exactly what I was trying to do. I'm sure you told on me."

No, I didn't. Everybody within two blocks of Aldridge's Barber Shop could've heard that glass crack.

I got to wondering.

If she *had* hit me with that rock, and if I had been hurt, or killed even, would she have been arrested and locked up in her own jailhouse home? Probably not. She was always the pet of the family.

I drove up the little alley in front of the now abandoned jail the other day. Guess what? A shattered glass at the front door still stands as mute testimony of the dastardly deed that a little sister tried to perpetrate on – I'm pretty sure of this – an innocent brother.

Perfect? She's a good one to be talking.

She admitted this too. She was about fourteen when she got this wild idea that she and her visiting girlfriends could climb that rickety fire escape ladder to the roof of the old abandoned jail, which faced the town square. It was a three-story building that backed up to the new jail, our home. The roof would afford a view clear down to Herbert Leigh's house on Wren Road, not to mention the bird's eye view of the town square.

My sister claimed they went up on that roof to sunbathe.

In truth it was not a suntan or a view they were after as much as it was to see which boys were driving round and round the town square. My sister admitted as much. If the boys had had feathers they'd have fluffed them. Round and round the square, and where they went was nowhere, but it was part of the courting ritual of small Southern towns fortunate enough to have squares.

I was upset when I heard about the roof forays. Not because they were dangerous, which they were. It's just that I never thought of doing it myself.

If girls could get up there, boys could too. And girls rode round and round the square in their own courting ritual.

Regrettably, Mom and Dad never found out about Patsy's high-flying escapades. I surely would've tried to sit in on a scolding that would've afforded me all kinds of teasing material and another chance to dodge a rock.

You might imagine that living in the jail would cut down on visits by our friends and classmates. No. They were eager to visit and didn't mind inviting themselves over to see what the inside of a jail looked like. Patsy's jail home did, however, put a damper on her overnight visitors. Sleeping in the county jail wasn't particularly appealing, but a few of her braver friends tried it anyway.

One of Patsy's good friends and classmates was Mary Jane Highsmith. She lived in a funeral home a block away from the jail. Her daddy, J. H. Highsmith, was the county coroner and operated the only funeral home in town. She'd ask Patsy to spend the night. Not on your life. There were dead bodies in that house!

Patsy would ask Mary Jane to spend the night with her. No way. There were criminals in that house! So it never happened.

As a teacher in the journalism program at Auburn, usually about halfway through the semester, once I pretty much had the students believing I was a decent guy, I would tell them there was a side of my life I had not revealed.

"A part of my teen years was spent in jail," I'd say, then dismiss the class. Hands would fly up; faces looked stunned; and I'd walk out of the classroom. At the next class session, students were determined to learn what crime I had committed.

"One lesson of journalism," I would say, "is do not assume." And then I'd tell them how I ended up living in the jail as the sheriff's son.

They're practicing journalists now. I hope they've not forgotten the lesson of the jail story. Oh, I know. They may have. Me forget? Never. I've been carrying jail stories with me for fifty years and they only get better with age.

Like the time... Wait a minute! There are just some things you don't put in a book.

Chapter 10

The Preacher Man

Nobody could make sense of this nondescript man, but everybody was talking about him.

It was just a case of adultery and two charges of assault and battery. On paper they looked like standard stuff, about as benign as many of the other hundreds of charges that had brought new guests to our home, the jail.

But these were different.

One, the man charged was a preacher.

Two, his visitors at the jail were a succession of attractive young women.

The mulberry bench, by now comfortably unelectrified, sagged under the weight of the growing number of older men who would sit there, whittle, and gossip – and watch the jail entrance. They would nudge each other as the attractive visitors entered the jail to see their cult leader, whose picture and story had been front-page items in the area's two major daily newspapers and in the local weekly.

The followers, nearly all women, would visit their cult leader often in the spring of 1952, and each Sunday they would gather back at the jail to sing and, as they described it, "pray him out of jail."

"Sheriff, what if they really do pray the jail doors open?" a newsman asked my dad.

My dad laughed. "If that happens, he's a free man."

The mulberry bench bunch weren't the only ones asking how the preacher man could pull into his fold female followers so obviously above their leader in appearance.

Sherman Lancaster, fifty-four, of Town Creek, was a self-described "holiness" preacher. He sat stoically in his cell. "He's quiet as a mouse," my dad told the media. "We hardly know he's around."

If you had seen the preacher on the street, you might have guessed he had just come to town from plowing cotton. Nobody could make sense of this nondescript man, but everybody was talking about him.

Lawrence County was full of talk and conjecture (and snide comments) about the man and his followers, who numbered about two or three dozen.

Probate Judge Isaac Johnson went over to the Thrasher-Mitchell Barbershop on the south side of the square each morning to get a shave. With hot towels wrapped over his face, he would hear something like:

"What you going to do with that preacher man, judge?"

I doubt that he ever answered. He was the non-jury trial judge for Lancaster's case, which was set for just days ahead on May 12.

For the little town of Moulton it was a date highly anticipated. Finally, those with inquiring minds and voyeuristic inclinations would learn the sordid details of the cult leader and his flock.

Lancaster's troubles had officially started on April 16, 1952, when he was arrested on the adultery and assault charges. The adultery charge came when the father of one of his cult swore out a warrant against the preacher, accusing him of sleeping with his married daughter. The assault charges grew out of an accusation that he grabbed teenage girls and kissed them by force.

On trial day, Deputy Auburn Smith escorted Lancaster from his jail cell across the street to the second-floor courtroom of the courthouse. The preacher, who served as his own lawyer, entered the courtroom to shouts of "Praise the Lord!" from the dozen or more followers already in their seats.

Deputy Auburn Smith, left, leads the preacher man to trial on adultery and assault charges. (Microfilm image from the archives of *The Decatur Daily*)

Others in the courtroom were not disappointed if they were expecting the sleazy details.

For the next two hours they feasted on tales of "spiritual" wives and adulterous acts and ritualistic hands-on body "anointments" by the preacher and more shouts of "Praise the Lord!" from followers.

The preacher, father of seven children, told the judge he believed in "spiritual" wives and that the Bible teaches that it is wrong for a legitimately married man and wife to live together. Testimony revealed that his "spiritual" wife was the twenty-five-year-old woman whose father had sworn out the adultery warrant.

But did he actually have more than a "spiritual" wife in conflict with his own philosophy?

Indeed he did, according to testimony of several women who said they themselves had slept with Lancaster on several occasions. Others testified that Lancaster "greeted" women of his group by kissing them and that several of the women had separated from their husbands under the influence of the preacher's teaching. Others testified to his "anointing" practices.

Lancaster called several witnesses in his defense. Each had the exact same statement: "He is a man of God and can do no wrong."

Judge Johnson, saying that the religious aspects of the trial did not influence his decision, handed down a six-month sentence in the state pen, a $100 fine on the adultery charge, and a one cent fine for each of the assault charges.

Lancaster's "spiritual" wife let out a shriek when the judge handed down the sentence. A probation hearing was set for June 2. Probation was denied.

It was back to his now familiar jail cell. He would catch the "dog wagon" for Kilby Prison within days.

"It was a dejected Lancaster who made the short walk from the courtroom back to his jail cell yesterday," said *The*

Florence Times on June 3. "None of the dozen followers at the hearing went with him as he reentered his jail cell to begin serving his sentence."

My dad had noted that on the previous Sunday the group's "pray him out of jail" offerings were devoid of enthusiasm. "They may be losing faith," he said.

The preacher's dozen followers in the courtroom, so vocal in other hearings, were silent.

"Maybe he felt deserted for the first time," Dad told *The Florence Times*. "All of his followers were left behind in the courtroom and none made an attempt to comfort him. He still has plenty of visitors but even they seemed to lose a great deal of their enthusiasm toward the end."

By now I could tell my dad was tiring of the whole mess. Amusement had turned to disgust. He just wanted the preacher man to get out of his hair and out of his jail.

Even the mulberry bench bunch was losing interest.

Good riddance, everybody thought, as we awaited the arrival of the dog wagon from Kilby.

Not so fast. He wants a new trial. The judge said he would hold a hearing to decide if there was new evidence. There wasn't enough for a new trial, argued solicitor Earle Proctor. The judge agreed. Back to jail to await the dog wagon.

Hold it. Lancaster appealed this time to the state court of appeals for a new trial. He was granted bond.

Well, at least he was out of our home, the jail. The appeal was denied.

Back to jail? No, another probation hearing.

By this time everybody involved had had it up to here with this disgusting and seemingly never-ending episode. That may have been the prime factor in the next official ruling: Mr. Lancaster, we will grant you probation if you and your followers will just get the heck out of Lawrence County and out of the State of Alabama. Go back to where you came from. Well, that wasn't exactly how the decree was written, but that's what it meant.

Where he came from was Mississippi. I don't think anybody around the Lawrence County courthouse breathed easily until they knew he and his caravan had crossed the state line. Still, it was a shame to have to do our neighboring state that way.

Chapter 11

Screwdriver – Unlikely Hero

He had an eleven-year-old boy who looked eight, and he was expected to put him behind bars.

My heroes are people I respect, admire, and in some fashion wish to emulate in my own life. That's why Screwdriver is my hero. An unlikely hero, to be sure. But a real hero, nevertheless.

Let me tell you why.

Arrest records show that at least ten thousand prisoners went through the doors of the Lawrence County Jail during my dad's two terms as sheriff in the 1950s. One of them was Screwdriver, a small-for-his-age black kid from Courtland. He'd stolen forty-seven cents in change from a store in his hometown. He stayed with us one year.

He was eleven years old.

And apparently nobody knew what to do with him. The agencies that today would be lined up at the jail door waiting for my daddy to bring him in were noticeably absent that day. Yes, it was a different time then. But that didn't ease my father's frustration. He had an eleven-year-old boy who looked eight, and he was expected to put him behind bars.

"I'm not going to do it," he told my mother.

"Well, then what...?

"We will keep him here, but we're not going to lock up a kid that age."

What they did was to make him a member of the family, probably raising some eyebrows in that little Southern town. But the stubborn streak that my dad exhibited every now and then kicked in.

"If somebody complains, just tell 'em to see me."

Nobody ever did as far as I know.

And on that day a bond began developing between a surrogate white father and a little black kid who was supposed to be in jail. My mother became his surrogate mother.

Rarely did my parents become involved in the personal lives of prisoners; that just led to complications, they felt. And lest you think they were flaming liberals, they were just typical God-fearing Southern conservatives.

So it was with some surprise that I saw what was happening with Screwdriver. I am not surprised that they treated him with civility. They were not the least bit race-conscious when it came to treating people with respect.

But I was surprised at how willingly they became involved with their new charge, and in a very personal way too. Surprised at how he and my father could be seen walking side by side through the courthouse, meeting all the county officials and more than a few other courthouse visitors. Screwdriver was walking with his friend, the High Sheriff, and he was proud.

At those times, an infectious smile that revealed pearly white teeth just made him the favorite of everybody he came in contact with. He wasn't bashful and he wasn't a smart aleck either. He'd talk with you as long as you wanted to talk.

With free rein at the jail – his official status was trusty – he'd often walk around town, making friends and chatting up whoever had time.

Everybody knew Screwdriver. And adored him. His life in Courtland seemed long ago and far away.

"Oh, yeah, I knew Screwdriver," said a delivery truck driver for a furniture store during that time. "You'd see him around town all the time."

And then one day, by now fully acclimated to his new life, he decided it would be appropriate to have some pictures made of himself. Not backyard snapshots. He wanted real pictures, in color, those up close where you could see your face.

So he went upstairs to Bain Studios on the north side of the square and told Charles Bain the sheriff had sent him over to have his picture made.

Since everybody around the square by that time had learned how my daddy felt about the youngster, Screwdriver had no trouble selling the picture idea.

When the hefty bill came into the sheriff's office, my mother's eyes just about popped out.

"Screwdriver, you ordered a bunch of pictures? Why in the world would you do that?"

I don't know what Screwdriver's answer was, but I'll bet it was a dandy – he was good at explaining things like that. No matter, my mother stayed mad at him for at least two minutes, and then the thing was forgotten.

Screwdriver's "bedroom" was an unlocked second floor cell. But at night the whole family was locked in. After all, this was the county jail.

Screwdriver made friends with the prisoners the same way he did with anybody he met: very easily. He would stroll around on the third floor in the little walkway in front of the cells and visit. It didn't matter that he might be talking with a murderer or robber or bootlegger. He could, and did, talk to anybody. Some of them probably wished they could've had him as their lawyer. It wasn't long before

Screwdriver was the pet, the mascot, the friend of everybody in that jail, prisoner or otherwise.

When I visited my mother in her Florence nursing home, I always tried to steer the conversation to those halcyon days of the '50s, and especially to that year Screwdriver was with us. The mention of his name always brought a smile to her face, and she would tell me again what a wonderful, smart boy he was and how she cried when he left for the state juvenile detention center at Mt. Meigs.

"Whatever happened to Screwdriver?" she asked on one of my visits.

"Mama, I don't know. We don't even know his last name. The records are so old, and even if we could find them, they wouldn't use his nickname."

The truth was that anything could have happened to him. He would have been in his mid-sixties by that time if – and that was a big if – he were still alive.

The percentage of repeat juvenile offenders was so high that an educated guess would have been that he spent a lot of years in prison. My mother would have none of that. Not her Screwdriver.

Then she would remember the day he walked in the jail door, and how she called to my father, "Franklin, he's just a kid!"

And she remembered how she made sure he ate right, made sure he had warm clothes, made sure he had anything else a mother usually provides, including love and just enough discipline to convince herself she wasn't spoiling him.

She knew Screwdriver well enough to ask plenty of questions when he was seeking permission to carry through on some idea or wanted something, usually a little pocket change for ice cream.

"You had to be careful," my mother said. "That boy could just charm you out of your socks." The twinkle in her eye betrayed her annoyance. She admired that side of Screwdriver too.

The new school term was nearing. But if he was in jail could he legally go to public school? "Well, of course he can," my mother declared without asking anybody. And she started making preparations to enroll him in the black elementary school. He had no school clothes, no school supplies, just an eagerness to learn.

So she went over to V. J. Elmore's five and dime on the north side of the square and came home with pencils and notebooks and just about anything she could think of that her new student might need.

Then she took him over to a department store, one whose owner probably already was on a first-name basis with Screwdriver, and bought him new pants, shirts, a warm coat, and a cap to keep his head warm.

All this paid for out of her and my father's private bank account. It didn't matter. She wanted her little man to go off to school looking like he belonged.

Then she took him over to the black elementary school and enrolled him in the fifth grade.

"He was so smart," my mother remembered. "Made all A's."

When parents' day came, Screwdriver insisted my mother come as his "mother." No need to insist. She wouldn't have missed it. In the audience, a white spot in a sea of black, she beamed as her favorite student displayed his work. She probably shed a tear when Screwdriver introduced her, with obvious pride, to his classmates and their parents.

Perhaps for the first time, this precocious youngster was seeing what it meant that somebody really cared for him and his future. Saw what love could do. Saw a glimpse of what the other side of life might hold.

My mother and dad hoped so. For one year they made sure he was exposed to values that would serve him for a lifetime. But most of all they showered him with love.

His presence brought a ray of sunshine to the Lawrence County Jail. Everybody – cooks, deputies, trusties, all of us – seemed to notice that the days were a little brighter when Screwdriver was around. It seemed that our steps were a little lighter, our smiles a little more frequent.

Screwdriver had a way of touching other people's hearts.

We all dreaded the day it would end. We knew that sooner or later he had to leave. The wheels of justice grind slowly. But they do grind. When the order came down to transport him to the state juvenile facility at Mt. Meigs, it hurt more deeply than we thought it would.

A pall fell over the jail, and it rolled over everybody. Not just my father and mother. Screwdriver was everybody's son. A lot of people became his protectors during that year. That included the prisoners who offered their encouragement, who told him to act right and become somebody. The cooks wanted him to make sure he ate right at his new home.

My mother hugged him and cried. She had been dreading this day. My daddy may have shed a tear too, though he'd never let you know it.

So Screwdriver, near tears, slid into the backseat of that same big old black Ford squad car that had brought him to jail in the first place. Now, a year later, it was speeding down Highway 31 South, each mile taking him farther away from a life that previously existed only in his dreams. Who could blame him if all this really did feel like a dream?

Four hours later he was processed into the state juvenile detention center at Mt. Meigs.

My father and mother never saw him again.

We were left wondering whatever happened to this young man who charmed his way into our lives. Was he dead? In prison? Our hope of all hopes was that he was still living, perhaps retired after a successful career. The latter would have been my parents' prayerful hope too. I wasn't optimistic, however.

We started our search for Screwdriver with one big obstacle: Now, more than fifty years later, no one could remember his real name.

All we had was a nickname. A memorable one – how many people do you know named Screwdriver? – but still it was only a nickname for a kid you last knew a half-century ago. The first move was to visit the juvenile detention center at Mt. Meigs, which in Screwdriver's time was an all-black facility.

I dropped in on the center just off I-85 in early 2009. I was searching for any records that might give a clue as to what his real name was.

"The clerk would have that information," said a woman as I entered the administration building. She directed me to an office at the end of a hall.

I began explaining my request to the clerk, telling her of how this white sheriff and his wife in north Alabama in the 1950s had taken in and befriended a little black youngster who had been accused of stealing. As I talked I noticed four or five staff members had gathered around to listen to the story of Screwdriver. A man came out of a corner office. He was Wayne Booker, administrator of Institutional Services for the Alabama Department of Youth Services.

"No records of that era exist," he said. "I'm sorry. But I can tell you what Screwdriver did while he was here."

I learned that Screwdriver, like all the other juveniles there at that time, worked in the fields picking and chopping cotton and harvesting and tending other crops on the many thousands of acres the facility operated. On days he was not in the field, he was in school taking subjects like math, science, and English.

Administrator Booker drove me into the fenced area, pointing out buildings where Screwdriver might have lived or worked. I just could not imagine Screwdriver in a setting like that, but I *could* imagine that after a year he would've been practically running the place.

Then we tried to call everybody we knew in Screwdriver's hometown of Courtland – teachers, principals, and older businessmen, anybody who might have remembered him or that nickname.

"No, but we'll check around."

Phone call after phone call and still no results.

Until my brother-in-law Wyckoff decided to call an Army Reserve friend who had owned a hardware store in Courtland for years.

"The name is familiar," said Bert Pippin. "Let me think about it."

Later Pippin said he believed Screwdriver was the kid who stole something from a store in Courtland. He called a woman who he thought might be Screwdriver's sister.

Yes, she said, he went to Chicago many years ago, but she had not heard from him in a long time.

We still didn't know his fate, but we had a name: Robert Hayes. And that was a big, big breakthrough.

Actually we had two names; the other, we thought, must be his brother.

At this point I called a professional people-finder and security expert. I gave him what little information I had.

Two days later he called back.

"I am afraid Screwdriver is dead," he said. Those words were like a knockout punch to the stomach.

No!

"Some of the data just did not add up," he explained. "It seemed to be leading me in two different directions."

One call led to another, but we were going nowhere fast. By this time Wyckoff had made more than fifty calls. We at least wanted to know how Screwdriver had died, when and where he died, and what his life was like after he was released from Mt. Meigs.

One of Wyckoff's calls led to an elderly man in Courtland who remembered that another elderly man might have remembered Screwdriver. And that second elderly man thought he remembered that a man he used to know as Screwdriver lived in Chicago, and he was pretty sure he knew the name of the street.

Chicago is a right good-sized town. Wyckoff, persistent as always, enlisted the aid of AT&T. He obtained the telephone number of fifteen people named Hayes who lived on the street the elderly man had mentioned.

First call: "Hello. I'm trying to locate a man named Hayes who was once called Screwdriver."

"I'm not him."

Second call: "Hello. I'm looking for a Mr. Hayes who has the nickname of Screwdriver."

"You're talking to him," said the man on the other end of the line.

Yes! He's alive!

Wyckoff had found Screwdriver himself, Mr. Robert Hayes. He was sixty-eight years old, retired as a successful businessman, widower, five children, ten grandchildren, big Bears fan. (He lives a block and a half from Soldier Field.)

In the interest of protecting his privacy, I will not divulge his address. Just know that he lives in a nice neighborhood, across the street from the mayor of Chicago.

Prison? Are you kidding? The incident at that store those many years ago was the only – only – misstep that would have even come close to landing him in jail. Even the amount of his haul back then was a paltry forty-seven cents.

"That was the only thing I ever did that I could be arrested for," he said emphatically.

My mother would have been proud of her Screwdriver. She had a deep faith that he would turn out just fine. She never said, but I know this because I knew her. She did a lot of praying for Screwdriver over the many years since she tearfully bade him farewell. Never underestimate the power of a mother who has connections like hers.

I believe in God. I believe in Jesus. I believe there's a heaven. But I don't really know if people up there can look down and see things, like some people say. But Dad, if you can, I know you're proud. You too, Mom. The time you two spent with that young man influenced his life in so many ways. He said so. And I know he influenced your lives too, maybe more than you ever let on.

Two days after Wyckoff found Screwdriver, I was on the phone with him for a lot of "Do you remember?" questions.

He remembered, alright. He remembered that his stay with our family was among the best times of his life.

Except now it was no longer Screwdriver I was talking with. It was a Mr. Robert Hayes of Chicago. I was now speaking with a retired Chicago businessman. He had, to my surprise, kept that soft Southern voice that charmed so many as an eleven-year-old in the Lawrence County Jail.

"You can still call me Screwdriver if you want to," he said.

Now, however, that name seemed to no longer fit.

We settled on Robert.

It was clear from our conversation that he cherished his time with my dad. The feeling must have been mutual.

"He would sit down and talk to me every day," Robert said. "He'd say, 'Screwdriver, is there anything you want?'

and I'd say, 'No, there is nothing I want. I have everything I want.' He'd take me to the courthouse, and he and I would walk through the courthouse a lot of times. And a lot of times we'd get in the car and just ride. You see, he was a very nice man."

"My mother. What do you remember about her?"

"She treated me like a son. I remember how good she fed me. I think about that a lot."

And he revealed that he even had a recent dream about his stay with us, and it did involve food and my mother.

"Mrs. Smith said, 'Screwdriver, you better come here and get your dinner before somebody else eats it up,'" he said, describing the dream.

"So the food was good?"

"It was *real* good," he said.

But it was more than food that nourished young Robert "Screwdriver" Hayes. His fertile mind was soaking up values that he said he retains to this day. He felt it then. He knows it now.

"I learned so much while I was there," he said. "For one thing I gained a positive outlook on life. And I saw how people helped people, how people helped me. Another thing I learned was you have respect for people, all kinds of people."

Robert can't recall what he and my dad talked about when they were just driving around or when they were sitting alone in the sheriff's office.

Let me make a good guess. He was advising Screwdriver on the important things in life, honesty and hard work and Christian values. And if I know my dad he probably teased Screwdriver a little too, like asking him about a girlfriend, stuff like that. He could communicate with children as well as anybody I've ever known and with an elegance and profundity that would surprise you. Most folks would've said that this would be completely out of character for the "still-busting" sheriff. They didn't know him.

My dad figured Screwdriver out right off the bat, sensed his innate honesty despite the reason for his arrest. Otherwise, he never would have given him the freedom to roam within blocks of the jail. And Robert was proud of that freedom.

"I could do most anything I wanted to," he said. "I was just like a free kid. I could get a key and go in their house (the bottom floor of the jail), get a key and go watch TV. I could go anywhere in that house. They trusted me."

"They trusted me." That phrase and that word, *trust*, came up often as he remembered those days of long ago.

My parents trusted him to go to the courthouse, to visit around the surrounding square, to have full run of the living quarters. They trusted him to go to school and return home.

"Mrs. Smith would say, 'Now you come straight home from school.' She'd say that every day."

And he always did.

With the freedom came responsibility. And Screwdriver knew that, knew he had earned the confidence and trust of the two most important people in his life at that time, and maybe ever. And he was not going to blow it.

When you think about it, all that trust and responsibility is a pretty heavy load for an eleven-year-old, now perhaps closer to twelve, to carry on his shoulders. Screwdriver had fun, plenty of it. But I believe he sensed, as young as he was, that this was his chance, maybe his only chance, to turn his life in the right direction. My parents thought the exact same thing. If you had not known Screwdriver you would probably doubt his ability to grasp that notion. I didn't.

His fondest memories, he said, were his trips to the courthouse.

"Everybody knew me, and we'd sit around the court-house and talk, or we would talk on the courthouse lawn. All day, just talk."

Now what a picture that must have been. An eleven-year-old kid who was supposed to be in jail holding forth with folks two or three times his age. Nobody but Screwdriver could've pulled that off. I always felt he would have made a great politician.

Fear never seemed to enter his mind. He'd spend a lot of time on the third floor talking to prisoners. Their crime was of no concern to Screwdriver – a murderer was the same as a loiterer. They were all people, and that was good enough for Screwdriver.

"But weren't you a little bit afraid?"

"No. No. They weren't about to hurt me. See, they treated me like kin. They were not going to hurt me. No way."

And they didn't.

He became especially fond of one prisoner, though he could not remember his name.

"He put a tattoo of my initials on my arm," he said. "That thing stayed on my arm for a long time. He did it with some kind of pen he had. It was only in the past five or six years that it disappeared. And sometimes you can even see some of it now.

"He stayed in jail a long time," he said of his prisoner friend. "We became real good friends. I carried him cigarettes and different things."

And then came the day Screwdriver left for Mt. Meigs.

"It was the worst day of my life," he said.

A part of the reason, he said, was because he was leaving his home and he had no idea what the future held for him at Mt. Meigs. That caused a hurt deep inside, but not as much as the image that is still etched in his mind from that day fifty years ago.

"I saw your mother standing out there crying," he explained. "She was trying to hold it back, but she just couldn't. She hugged me and she cried and she said she was sorry that I had to go."

Life for us around the jail was empty after that. You'd still halfway expect Screwdriver to pop up from around the corner with that million-dollar smile and ask, "Mrs. Smith, how long 'til dinner's ready?"

It was a big change for Screwdriver too.

"When I first got to Mt. Meigs I worked in the fields," he remembered. "I would work a day in the fields and go to school a day, the fields one day and school the next. Then I got a job working in the little boys' dormitory."

Later he was assigned jobs in the "big boys'" dorm.

He is unsure of just how long he stayed in the detention center.

About five years, he guessed.

"Good grief, that was an awfully long time to keep you for such a minor offense, wasn't it?"

"It was a real long time. I stayed there so long I was just like a trusty. At that time they just kept you until they decided to let you go."

He described his stay there as positive, "a good experience." In fact, when they released him and he started high school in Moulton, the lady who ran the "little boys'" house enticed him to come back and help her. He did, for a year. It was during that time he found himself smack in the middle of historic times, and he became an active participant in them.

That was when a young Martin Luther King Jr. was pastor of Dexter Avenue Baptist Church in Montgomery. He was with Dr. King on marches, recoiled from police confrontations, and backed away from the dogs used to keep the marchers at bay. He took part in the Montgomery Bus

Boycott, walking to work across the capitol lawn on those days when he worked in Montgomery waiting tables.

Then he went back to Moulton and graduated from high school in 1959.

So how did he end up in Chicago? It wasn't because he'd lived through those trying days in Montgomery, he said.

"I just decided when I finished high school I was going to see my cousin and brother," he said.

His first job was as a bellhop at Holiday Inn at O'Hare International Airport. He drove a courtesy van from O'Hare to town and back. That lasted about five years, he said, and then he went into business for himself.

"I bought a beauty supply store," he said. "Ran that for several years and then retired after I came down with diabetes." His wife is deceased.

He had a little scare with prostate cancer a while back, but that seems to be under control now. Today his life is centered on his five children and ten grandchildren.

"The grandchildren are all about to have birthdays," he said, agreeing that Granddad was in for a busy time.

He would go to more Bears games if he could get tickets, he said, and he occasionally attends a White Sox or Cubs game. His favorite team: "They all are."

He comes back to Alabama each Thanksgiving, he said, to visit relatives in Courtland. But for the rest of the year Moulton and the Lawrence County Jail are but memories of a different age, a different world.

Still, he said he might just drive down to Auburn on his next visit to Alabama and spend a little time visiting the boy they called Jackie who came home to jail from college, maybe drive a few miles west over to Mt. Meigs to see if the old place had changed much, and then it would be nice to drive on over to Montgomery to see the civil rights monuments and museums.

"You know, I might just do that," he said.

"My parents would be thrilled if they knew I was talking to you at this moment," I told him.

"I would be thrilled if I could see them," he said.

Over the years, I have thought a lot about this youngster we called Screwdriver. He was a hero to me long before I knew the rest of the story – his confidence, his charisma, his amazing ability to adapt to a new world, his passion for life, his optimism, all the obstacles he overcame just in that one year at his jailhouse home.

How could he not be a hero to those whose lives he touched? How could you not admire and respect this man? How could you not wish to emulate a lot of what you've now learned about Robert "Screwdriver" Hayes?

To learn of his productive life over the past fifty years was a thrilling discovery.

The circle is now complete.

Of course, there are other heroes in this story.

Their names are Franklin and Ruby Smith.

Chapter 12

Our Own Little Miss Sunshine

She would jump from the car and dash to the front door, red hair flying, her freckled face beaming.

A lot of memorable characters passed through the doors of the Lawrence County Jail in the 1950s. Some were so drunk they were practically dragged in. Some were sullen and in handcuffs. And some just came in without incident and became a part of our extended family, especially the prisoners we called trusties. You've met Jackleg and Big Richard and Willie B. and, of course, Screwdriver.

Then along came Joyce. She wasn't a prisoner, but she may have been the favorite of our old girl, the county jail, because she brought so much joy and happiness inside those gray walls. My dad with his little come-to-visit passenger would drive up the alley in front of the jail. She would jump from the car and dash to the front door, red hair flying, her freckled face beaming.

Like Screwdriver, Joyce White practically became a member of our family after my father met her during his second campaign for sheriff. She was three years old and lived with an aunt and uncle. She belonged in a Norman Rockwell painting.

Buddies. Dad and Joyce

She stole my dad's heart the minute he saw her playing in her driveway that early spring day in 1954 when he was hunting votes in the Five Points community of eastern Lawrence County. My dad always had a soft heart for kids, and it was just like him to say something like, "How would you like to come spend the night with us in the jail?" Her aunt and uncle, the Coy Whites, knew my dad's reputation for honesty and decency. They had no apprehension about letting their niece do that. Today, all kinds of red flags would be flying.

Joyce never forgot that invitation, nor did my mom and dad, and for the next four years in the jail (and for years afterward) Joyce was my little sister and she looked to Patsy as her big sister. In the eyes of my mom and dad, she could do no wrong. I think they loved her as much as they did Patsy and me.

"May I skate now?" she would ask my mother.

"Yes, but don't you go outside."

And in minutes the metal skate wheels would clack across the tiled floor of the jail's bottom floor. I can see her zipping perilously close to a recoiling trusty with a mop bucket as she darts around a blind corner. She brought an exuberance and innocence to a building that housed losers and miscreants. She brought us, the sheriff's family, happiness and laughter and the joy of loving one of God's little angels as if she were our own.

Joyce, now Joyce Peters of Moulton, remembers her visits with us at the jail as "wonderful."

"I came to visit and got out of the car on those loose gravel and I'd just run in the front door," she remembered. "I couldn't wait to get there. The jail was big and different. It became a special place where you had fun, but most of all you felt love. It was where as a little girl I had someone else to love me. I felt loved *and* wanted. They [the family] made me feel special."

And yes, she admitted, Mom and Dad did a good job of spoiling her. Ice cream and candy and trips to the soda fountain at Sandlin's Rexall Drug Store had a way of doing that.

"Mother and Daddy doted on her like she was some little queen," Patsy said. "She was never ready to go home. Daddy had to promise her he would come after her again in a few days."

Unlike "big sister" Patsy, she was unafraid of the jail. "I felt well protected," she said. "But I was never allowed to go upstairs where the prisoners were."

It took fifty years for that to happen. Even then not a prisoner was in sight.

In June 2009 Joyce, now a licensed practical nurse at a Decatur nursing home and a grandmother herself, was invited to visit the old jail again along with my dad's three grandchildren and four great-granddaughters.

Current sheriff Gene Mitchell, who as a youngster had known of my father, led us upstairs in the now all but abandoned old jail. We eased through dusty dark rooms of peeling olive green paint, past rusting bunks enclosed by rusting cell bars and heavy steel doors. Except for the echoes of emptiness, that was about all that was left of our once proud home, a home once clean and sparkling and alive, even up here where the prisoners lived.

What was Joyce thinking as we threaded our way through and around the aging cellblocks? I wondered. I do know that she got an eyeful, as did the grandchildren and great-grandchildren, but she said little. It was as if she was thinking, *So this is what I wasn't allowed to see. I didn't miss much.* Wrong.

"I was thrilled," she said later. "I had wondered all those years what it was like up there." There were no surprises, she said, except one. "It was so much smaller than I had imagined it to be."

The first floor, where she skated and did pretty much anything else she wanted to do, seemed much smaller too than she remembered. Like my own reaction, she said she had a hard time making this place look and feel like the home she once knew. But then that was to be expected. Stay away fifty years and your mind begins to lose some of the details, like how big the place really was.

Still, warm memories came flooding back, Joyce said. Among the fondest was her relationship with Mom and Dad. She remembered my mother as "a sweet and loving person."

"She made me some of the cutest clothes." And lots of them too, she said. She remembers that Mom always put ruffles on them.

"I don't know who enjoyed them more, whether it was Mother making them or Joyce wearing them," Patsy said. "She probably got a new dress every week or so."

What does she remember about my dad, whom she called "Uncle Franklin"? "He would spoil you," she laughed, admitting that she probably did have him wrapped around her little finger. "I would look up into his eyes, and his eyes alone told me that he'd do just about anything I asked."

She and Patsy became best pals in a big-sister, little-sister kind of way.

"I wanted to be like Patsy," she said. "She was pretty, and I looked up to her."

Patsy said, "She always slept with me when she came and never gave any kind of problem about going to bed, probably because we let her stay up two hours past her normal bedtime. She always kissed me before she went to sleep. Oh, how I loved her!"

Patsy remembers that Joyce obeyed "like a little soldier." Fifty years later Joyce said that was because she didn't want to disappoint anybody by acting up. No mystery to that; she wanted to be invited back.

Joyce loved to go into the kitchen and watch the cooks. She got to help set the table, stir the food, and put ice in the tea glasses.

"She really liked helping put the big food tray on the dumbwaiter and sending the meals up to the prisoners," Patsy said. "I don't think she ever figured out how it worked."

When Mom worked in the sheriff's office at the courthouse, Joyce would go along and play "secretary."

"I'll bet she used one hundred sheets of paper drawing pictures every time she went," Patsy said.

I don't think the taxpayers of Lawrence County would have cared.

**Joyce was flower girl at
Patsy's and Wyckoff's wedding.**

Her sharpest memories, Joyce said, are of Patsy's and Wyckoff's wedding in 1957 at Moulton Baptist Church. That's because she was the flower girl, seven years old at the time, and wearing a dress my mother had made for her.

"That dress was the prettiest thing I had ever seen," she said.

"She looked like a little doll," Patsy said, describing the dress as "white and beautiful."

"Mother bought her new white shoes and socks to go with the dress and made her a beautiful headband out of the dress material and put fresh flowers on it. She was the proudest person at the wedding – and by far the cutest."

"The rehearsal went fine," Joyce said. "But when I saw all those people in the church at the wedding, I was scared to death."

She performed her duties at the wedding flawlessly. You knew she would. The flower girl was not about to disappoint her big sister.

Patsy and I have talked of how much we were blessed because that little girl came into our lives, of how much pleasure our parents received in doting on their new little daughter, of how lucky we were that our dad made that campaign stop at the White residence a half-century ago.

Luck? Not in Joyce's mind.

In a voice as soft as that of a little girl of fifty years ago, she put it this way: "God has a way of bringing people together."

Chapter 13

Speaking Personally

On that day I gained a new appreciation for my dad; I was seeing a side of him I never knew existed.

When I told my fifteen-year-old granddaughter Maggie that my father never told me he loved me, she was aghast.

But here's the thing. I'm almost sure that not one father among our Mt. Hope neighbors ever told one of their children flat out, "I love you." I'm sure the mothers did. My mother did. But not fathers. It just wasn't done.

Maggie and others of her age may have trouble understanding that. Her daddy constantly tells her and her sister Claire he loves them. Their mother Lynn does too. So do their grandparents. We are all a little more touchy-feely now. I applaud that.

So I accept the fact that my father grew up in a vastly different world than did my son. And he would not even be remotely familiar with the world his great-granddaughters are growing up in now.

So he never out and out said, "I love you." He didn't have to. I felt his love in so many different ways. He paid for my college education with never a complaint or question. He trusted me to do the right thing. And he let me know he loved me by the Christian life he lived. Perhaps most importantly, he never said or did anything that indicated he did *not* love me.

There were times when he tried to openly express his emotions in our relationship. It was not easy for him. An example may suffice.

My high school baseball team was playing a team from Huntsville. Their pitcher was fast, real fast. We were waving at air all day. Somehow we managed to tie the game, and in the bottom of the ninth inning we had a man on second base. Guess who came to bat? One of the weakest hitters on the team. Me.

I know the coach was wishing he had somebody, anybody, to pinch hit. I started swinging about the time the ace was winding up. The ball struck my bat. Where did that come from? The ball sailed over second base, and the winning run came home. I had already noticed that my dad's squad car was parked some distance away from the field, and I was aware he was watching me play. That was a thrill because he seldom had the time to attend my basketball or baseball games. And this day was really special. He would be proud, I thought. When I looked again the car had gone.

When sometime later he arrived back at the jail:

"Y'all played baseball today."

"Yes, sir, we played Huntsville."

He stammered just a bit trying to think of what to say next.

Come on, I was thinking, *put your arms around me and say, "Great game; I'm proud of you."* He wanted to do that, I'd bet on it, but he just couldn't pull the trigger.

He said instead, "Can I buy you a Coke?"

I understood. No sweat.

The times he would ask me to ride with him on patrol were special. We might not have talked a lot, but it was fun being with him, and I think he enjoyed being with me.

It was on one of these trips that we saw a young couple in a fight. And it would lead to a jaw-dropping reaction on my part because of my dad's skill in dealing with them, including a marriage counseling session that would have done the professionals proud.

We were just below Wheeler Dam in the northern part of the county on a sunny spring day, a day in which many people were out enjoying the water and the park. We sat in the car overlooking the mile-long width of the beautiful Tennessee River.

"Would you look at that!" my father said, straightening in his seat. He wasn't talking about the river.

A young man and woman, a husband and wife it turned out, were about one hundred yards from us along the water's edge on one of the many large limestone rocks in that area. He slapped her. She countered with a punch to the head. He flailed. She flailed. And on it went until we were there to stop it.

My father put the man in the car with us and told the wife to follow us in their car. We ended up at Moulton in the sheriff's office. He told them he really hated to put them in jail but that what they were doing was a clear-cut case of assault and battery. They nodded.

He stressed family values and how marriages were based on understanding and trust and the joy of children and of all the wonderful things in store for them – if they treated each other with respect. They listened attentively. They had little choice.

My father again told the couple how much he hated to put them behind bars but that the law was the law.

Finally, he wondered if he let them off this time if they'd ever treat each other that way again.

"No, sir. No. Absolutely not."

"Well, then, here's what I'm going to do…"

The embarrassed couple left, the relief evident on their faces. My dad, of course, never intended to put them in jail. I thought, *My goodness, was that my father talking?* On that day, I gained a new appreciation for my dad; I was seeing a side of him I never knew existed.

The most memorable patrolling trip I ever made with him was one Saturday night in late spring of 1954. That trip revealed more evidence that the civil rights movement was stirring from its infancy. We had read about unrest in some Northern cities, including Detroit.

I was home from school on a weekend visit. I was just completing my sophomore year at Auburn.

"We're going to check out some pretty rough places," my dad said. "You might want to take this along." He handed me an automatic .32-caliber pistol. I slipped it into my right front pocket.

Our first stop was a little restaurant along Alabama Highway 20 between Decatur and Courtland. We had no more than parked when we spotted a black man with an outstanding warrant against him. He was a gentle man – we knew him from previous arrests. My father, I'm sure, had just as soon we hadn't happened upon him. The charge was for a minor offense anyway. "Now that he's here, we might as well take him in," my daddy said.

Those were days of segregation. Our prisoner was not allowed inside the restaurant.

"Jackie, you stay out here and watch him while I go see what's going on inside."

The prisoner and I sat in front of the restaurant, leaning back against the concrete block wall. We were having a pleasant conversation when I noticed a shiny black 1954 Chevrolet with Michigan plates pull into the parking area.

I gave it little more than a passing glance.

I looked up to see a tall black man standing over me.

"What the h- - - is going on here?" he said.

"Well, sir," I said, "I don't really think that's any of your business."

Wrong answer.

He picked up my 135-pound body with both hands and slammed me against the concrete block wall. My head snapped backward. I can only imagine that I slid down that wall like a flattened cat in a cartoon.

I was on the ground when I regained my senses. My dad was aiming his pearl-handled .38 revolver at the man who'd done his son wrong.

I got to my feet and moved toward the man.

"Daddy, don't!"

"Move out of the way, Jackie." As he moved around to get a clear line of sight, I moved a little more toward the man he was aiming at. My dad had that fiery look in his eyes.

"Daddy, please don't. It's not worth it. Daddy, please!"

The man's passengers were out of the car now, yelling at my father, making threatening gestures, creating mayhem. Their driver stood frozen. He apparently was convinced that if he moved away from me he'd be shot. I have absolutely no doubt he would have been. In the commotion, the passengers sped away in the black Chevrolet.

Finally, my dad lowered his pistol. He holstered it, took out his handcuffs, popped them on the perpetrator, and shoved him into the squad car. We took him to jail and learned who his companions were and where they were staying. We spent the rest of the night hunting them down in Decatur with the help of city police.

Our first prisoner slipped into the night. Jail for him would have to wait.

I had forgotten that dad had given me the pistol until I found it when I undressed for bed (an empty cell) the next morning. I went to sleep easily despite a mild headache that had disappeared by the time I awakened that afternoon.

The only disagreement I had with my dad after he became sheriff taught me a lesson I was never to forget.

My dad had sold me a 1950 white Ford for $200 plus a small monthly payment, the amount of which I do not recall. It wasn't much of a car and it wouldn't run very fast, but it was a car. I don't know where I got the $200 down payment. Maybe it was from money I had saved from work with a newspaper. I don't know. He knew that I'd never be able to pay off that car, and I knew he knew. So I didn't worry about it.

I was a high school junior at the time, an age where I was extremely knowledgeable – there wasn't much I didn't know, and I was entitled to all the good things that my parents were providing me.

My father wanted to borrow my car.

"No, sir," I said. "I've got a date tonight. I need my car."

"Jackie, we will be on a stakeout. I don't want to use a squad car that everybody will recognize. I need your car."

I argued. He wouldn't relent.

Finally, I said words that have been echoing in my ears for the 50 plus years since then.

"Well, if that's the way you're going to be, just give me my money back and keep the car!"

He whipped out his checkbook, wrote me a check for $200, got my keys and walked out the door.

I knew immediately how utterly stupid, how utterly arrogant, were my actions. Only my pride kept me from calling my dad back before he reached the door.

I sat there dumbstruck, staring at a piece of paper, no car and a date down the road expecting me to be there in 30 minutes.

Let's be honest. I don't remember who the date was with, or even if I finally made it to her door that night. That is no longer important. What was important is the way I acted, and I vowed then never to be such a spoiled brat again.

Whether that turned out to be the case is open to debate. My dad and I eventually worked things out. He knew he had taught me a lesson.

A few days later he tossed me the keys. He said not one word. He didn't have to.

Strange thing about that car. I never enjoyed driving it again.

Mom and Dad weren't big socializers, but they didn't mind getting all dressed up for the wedding of their daughter. At least Mom didn't.

Patsy recognized our dad's peculiarities when it came to the relationship with his son and daughter.

"No," she said, "he never told me he loved me, but I knew he did. There was never a doubt about that – ever. He was always so good to me. I thought he was the most honest person I ever knew and he lived an exemplary life before us. I was extremely proud of him."

She recalls how she may have been the best customer the Fay Lee dress shop had, coming home with the latest fashions on a regular basis. Mom and Dad, of course, had to foot the bill.

My dad would see her wearing a new outfit and with a sigh of inevitability would say, "Well, I guess I'll see how much it costs when the cancelled checks come in."

"He never complained," Patsy said.

As I had yearned for my parents' presence at my high school basketball and baseball games, so did Patsy as a cheerleader for the Lawrence County High School Red Devils.

She was a cheerleader for four years and never did my mom or dad make it to one of her games.

"I dreamed of them sitting in the stands watching me," she said. "He would have one of the deputies take me to the home games and come back and get me. But before every game he would say to me, 'Is your uniform ready?' So I knew he wanted me to look my best.

"I guess things are different now. We live in different times. Wyckoff and I never missed a home game at Alabama during the three years Suzanne was a cheerleader, and we never missed a game in high school, home or away."

So what does she think of her daddy who never came?

"I thought I had the most perfect daddy in the world."

You may not understand how that could be. Her granddaughters Reagan and Ruby may not now comprehend the complexities of our relationship with our father in those days a half-century ago. To Patsy's everlasting credit, she did. She could see deeper, could see beyond his no-shows at her games, could see love when others may have been too wrapped up in their own egos to notice or care. I love my sister for a lot of reasons. How she handled her relationship with our dad is one of them.

Just about the time you got good and aggravated at Dad, he would do something to make you realize the deep-down goodness of the man.

Patsy recalls how kind he was to prisoners when he would arrest them.

She would listen as he gave them his little talk about how they should straighten up, quit selling whiskey, or quit drinking, or quit whatever it was they were charged with.

"I do believe he had an influence on many of them," she said. "I don't think he ever made an enemy by talking with them about doing right. He probably never knew it, but that really made an impression on me. I thought, *What a courageous man to talk to the 'bad' people of the county in that manner.* And he was sincere, because he was a Christian himself."

Patsy was also appreciative of how our dad treated her many friends who visited her at the jail.

"Daddy was always so sweet and kind to them and made them welcome. I felt so special to have him as a daddy. Of course, he always had to tease them about something."

Edwin Smith was among the young people who visited the jail a number of times, though not as one of Patsy's classmates.

He and his father, Malcolm, visited my father often when they were in Moulton. Malcolm was my dad's nephew. My dad and Malcolm would talk of recent raids or arrests, and young Edwin soaked it all in.

"As a young boy, some of my best times were the visits to see Uncle Franklin," he said. "I think he may have been my dad's favorite uncle. I know they were close. [My dad] did not look up to many people, but he looked up to Uncle Franklin. I did too."

Those visits had one negative.

"I was scared of that jail," he said. "Uncle Franklin would ask me if he could take me upstairs to see the cells, and I'd just shake my head no."

Perhaps the most amazing thing about those visits though was that they didn't end there.

Young Edwin would go home and put on paper what he heard discussed. The result is that he captured much of the flavor and essence and mindset of his uncle, the sheriff.

On one of those visits, he heard his father and the sheriff talking about the notorious Dawson gang that operated in the next county. That gang was criminal big-time – killings, illicit liquor operations, illegal activities of nearly every sort. They were named in the aforementioned movie, *Walking Tall*, as the gang that could wipe out Sheriff Buford Pusser, the subject of the Tennessee-based movie.

So when young Edwin heard "Dawson" his mind snapped to attention.

I have no doubt that what young Edwin recorded is true; it reinforces my belief, and that of a lot of others, that my father the sheriff had no fear.

My father had gotten word that the Dawsons were intending to set up a bootlegging operation in the little community of Wolf Springs, just inside Lawrence County and near their base of operations in Colbert County.

"The Dawsons were a rough bunch; people were being shot over there. It would be a matter of time before they decided to test [Uncle Franklin]," Edwin explained.

"He slipped across the county line [one night] to their house and waited for Pride Dawson, the leader of the gang, to come out. When he did Uncle Franklin cornered him. After their little talk, [Dawson] agreed not to set up shop in Lawrence County. Uncle Franklin told Pride that the next visit would not be a social call. They never moved into Lawrence County!"

I'm sure my dad never had in mind to become the Wyatt Earp of Lawrence County. There is no doubt he felt a responsibility to the people who elected him, and he pursued his duties with a passion that created both enemies and loyal supporters.

His enemies weren't hard to identify. He either put them in jail, or he put their friends or family in jail, or he wouldn't look the other way when a political power figure asked him to.

On the other hand, he built relationships that remained strong well after he left office and until his death.

Among his best friends and most ardent supporters was Dr. Edwin Carpenter of Courtland. Dr. Carpenter, a family practitioner, set up an office in September 1949, a little less than two years before my father took office.

He became a beloved figure in Courtland during his more than four decades of practice. But the start was rough. That's where my dad came in.

Dr. Carpenter told Brette Martin of *The Moulton Advertiser* in October 1996:

"This was a rowdy little town when I moved here.

"The last time I really had a group of traumatic injuries, both gunshots and knife wounds, I had 11 at one time. There was a storm, and the power was going off and on. I had to use candlelight, but I made it through patching them all up. Of course, I had to go around tying off all the bleeders before I could finish each one.

"This was about the time Sheriff Franklin Smith came into office and I was most unhappy with the fighting. I was about ready to leave. I'll never forget him saying, 'Will you give me two weeks to clean this town up?'

"I just couldn't believe him but I agreed to give him a chance. That was the last rowdy-type incident I had to deal with. He dried this town up in two weeks.

"He was a remarkable man."

Chapter 14

Times That Tried Our Souls

He was losing what was most dear to him...and he was helpless to stop it.

Storm clouds started gathering over my father's tenure as sheriff on Thursday, October 4, 1956. My father was never the same after that day. He fought hard to keep what he truly valued: his good name and reputation. And they were very nearly destroyed by the ill winds that followed.

On that day five miles south of Courtland, four men were running off a batch of moonshine. Unknown to them, federal ATU agents and my father lurked in the woods, watching from their vantage points, ready to strike.

They waited until the men had poured 2,000 pounds of sugar into the four 1,500-gallon-capacity stills that made up the big operation. Then they moved in for the arrests.

They nabbed three men. The fourth man tore through the woods. He was arrested three days later at his mother-in-law's house in a small community a few miles east of Courtland.

The man was Sam Gilmore. He had worked as a deputy for my dad for a short time. My dad had fired him for conduct deemed unfit for an officer of the law. As was his nature, my dad never revealed what that conduct was.

Sam Gilmore was the brother of two of my father's deputies, Roy Gilmore Jr. and Harold Gilmore. My father opted not to tell the deputies that the raid was to take place, a raid the revenuers and my dad were fairly sure would net their brother. The deputies were furious.

Court testimony later revealed they cursed my dad and threatened to kill him. They denied that.

My dad fired them. They said they "quit for reason." The net result was that they were gone three weeks later.

At the time, my sister, mother, and I were vaguely aware that issues of trust had been developing between my father and Roy Jr. and Harold Gilmore. But my father never went into the details of those problems. We could tell he wasn't as open with the deputies as before, didn't discuss with them intimate details of what he had learned from informants. We could also tell that something was weighing heavily on his mind.

When I read a story of the raid in the local paper and saw that the sheriff's force wasn't involved, I thought, *Uh-oh, something's going on here.* I realized that my dad was in a corner. If he had told the brothers of the plan and it turned out to be a fruitless operation, he would have to answer to the ATU agents he had worked with on the raid. If he did not tell the deputies, he was sure to incur their wrath. So he chose the latter, a decision that was entirely predictable.

Sam Gilmore was freed on $2,000 bond. He was to go before a federal grand jury in Birmingham the next February. He was charged with ownership and possession of an illegal distillery.

In the ensuing months, like a lighted match dropped in dry sedge grass, rumors that the sheriff was taking payoffs to protect moonshiners began sweeping the county.

It was the topic of conversation in all the hot spots for gossip – coffee shops, diners, barbershops, beauty shops – from one end of the county to the other. For a while, we were blithely unaware of the rumor storm sweeping the county.

Patsy, my mother, and I finally caught on. My dad was caught in the middle of the storm but said nothing to us. We were confounded. We, of course, did not believe for an instant that Dad was taking payoff money.

In the past several months in research for this book, I talked to a half-dozen people who knew my father, perhaps better than I did, politically, and in some ways better than I did personally. I had been away for four years, not really paying close attention to what was going on with the sheriff's office. Tell me the truth, I asked those who knew him best. Don't sugarcoat anything. Each told me they never put any stock in the rumors.

"Your dad didn't take any payoffs," one told me.

Hayden Coffey, my dad's old friend and confidant, assured me that Dad never did and never would take money from bootleggers and moonshiners.

"They wanted him out of office," he said.

Later, influential leaders in the county who wanted to continue the war against moonshine asked Coffey to run for sheriff.

"After what they did to Franklin, I wouldn't even consider it," he said.

Others, who didn't know dad as well, said yes, they had heard the rumors back then. "I don't know if they were true," one said. "But, yes, I heard them." Fair enough. If I had not been so close to the situation, had I not known the character of my dad, I might have had wondered too. So I hold no grief for those who might have doubted.

To my father's enemies, and he had plenty, this was it – the time to turn the pack dogs loose. I was told in doing my research that moonshiners, now that my dad was in effect a wounded prey, had moved in for the kill with renewed vigor. Part of that was to pour money into the upcoming campaign against him.

Or was it just plain old rough-and-tumble Lawrence County politics in which anything goes?

Whatever the reason, my dad was hurting inside. You could tell it in his demeanor, in his attitude, in his dealing with the rest of the family with whom he was even less talkative than usual.

We hurt for him. Six great years for him, for us, and for the people of the county were going up in smoke. He was losing what was most dear to him – his good name and reputation – and he was helpless to stop it. Saying it wasn't true, which he did, had little effect. The flames were out of control.

At the time, my father's mother, Maggie, lay deathly ill at her daughter Susie Roberson's home in Mt. Hope. My father gathered at her bedside, as did other members of the family. Dad placed his hand on her forehead.

"Mama," he said, "I swear to you that I have never taken a dime in payoffs."

She died shortly thereafter, on February 28, 1958, at age eighty-five. I learned of this incident just months ago. At first I was surprised. It didn't seem like something my father would do. He normally let criticism and accusations go without comment. That he wanted to assure his mother of his innocence before her death was an indication of just how deeply the rumors were eating at him.

I do not intend to make the situation more dramatic than it was, but to a family whose lives were built around Christian values, we were in crisis mode, one that cried out for a response. But we had no response; we were helpless to calm the storm that swirled around us.

A pall settled over the jail, once bustling with laughter and optimism. We needed Cora's laughter and Screwdriver's smile and Joyce's hugs.

And we needed the truth.

All this was coming at a time when my father was laying the groundwork for a run at a third term.

The prospects looked bleak. We didn't know the half of it.

My dad still held out hope though. He told his nephew, Horace Smith, that he could still turn things around. Horace was doubtful and told him so. Our closest friends and supporters privately told us to expect the worst.

The former deputy's arrest for moonshining was just another arrow in the enemy's arsenal. As it turned out, Sam Gilmore's arrest would lead to much, much more than that.

In February, candidates started lining up to run for the sheriff's office. Regarded as the strongest was Claude Lee Terry, forty-nine, who worked for three years as a deputy for my dad. He was expected to be the favorite in the valley region of Courtland and Town Creek, where he grew up. Others in the field were fifty-four-year-old Neal Fretwell of Moulton, a former deputy sheriff, though never on my dad's staff; former sheriff J. K. Ayers of Moulton, no age given, who served one term as sheriff, 1931-1934; and Lester Reed, fifty-six, of Moulton, a veteran policeman and former deputy on my dad's force.

Ordinarily, that slate would not represent much of a threat. But now, with the incumbent crippled, they appeared more than formidable.

As the campaign moved toward the May 6, 1958, primary, rumors of payoffs, now joined by other rumors of the vilest nature, continued to plague Dad's campaign.

By now, we, the family, had conceded the election in our minds. My dad had not, and the primary totals for the top two were surprisingly close. Terry led with 1,994 votes. My father was second with 1,821. The runoff was June 3.

But we also knew this: My father had gotten about all the votes he was going to get in the primary. Given the bitter nature of the campaign, voters were either strongly against my dad or avid supporters. Terry, we felt, was going to get nearly all the votes first cast for the other three candidates in the primary.

Politics are such slick and sometimes sleazy animals that you can never pinpoint political shenanigans with a 100 percent degree of confidence. You can, however, record what you do know and make a reasoned judgment from what you know to be true.

This was true: On Saturday and Sunday, May 24 and 25, eight days before the runoff election, federal agents moved into Lawrence County without notifying my dad and charged thirteen people with violation of Internal Revenue Service laws, meaning they paid no federal tax on the homemade hooch they were accused of selling.

ATU agents told the media they had broken up an organized ring of illegal whiskey dealers. One man, they said, greeted them, these perfect strangers, told them to come on in, and without question or fear of arrest went out back to get the moonshine they presumably came to buy. I was suspicious of that statement. I never knew of a bootlegger that dumb. The intent, with words like "whiskey ring" in newspaper headlines, obviously was to make my father look bad. The story added fuel to the anti-Smith fire.

I read the names of those arrested. Most of them were two-bit bootleggers who had been arrested often by my father and his deputies. One man arrested was a business-man who, while he might take a drink on Saturday night, would never be a part of some illicit ring. I had known this man and his family for years.

Since the raid was timed, in our strong opinion, to influence the election, and since it was obviously hyped well beyond its significance, our family had begun to wonder when the other shoe would drop. Given the arrest of Sam Gilmore and the firing of his two brothers as deputies, it didn't take a genius to figure that something was going on behind the scenes.

Meanwhile, my dad went about campaigning in a race he had little chance of winning. He lost to Terry big-time, 3,720 to 2,193 – a 1,527-vote margin. His home community of Mt. Hope went for him again, although not by as large a margin as before.

Election night had all the earmarks of a wake – a few smiles, a few laughs, but mostly questions of how things could have gone so wrong so quickly. My dad was sitting on the mulberry bench, accepting condolences without rancor. Like us, he had known deep down what was coming.

A drunk came wobbling down the alley in front of the jail. "Franklin," he slurred, "you're the best d--- sheriff this county ever had. I just want you to know, old buddy, that I supported you all the way."

My dad smiled weakly and shook the man's out-stretched hand. On another day at another time, this election night partier might have been jailed for public drunkenness. Not tonight.

So the new sheriff would take office the following January. That left my dad seven and a half months to prepare for a new life. First off was to build a home just east of Moulton along what the City of Moulton later named Franklin Smith Road.

Not yet fifty, he had to start preparing for another way to make a living.

Still, rumors persisted. This time the rumor was that brothers Sam, Roy Jr., and Harold Gilmore, the ex-deputies, would testify against my dad before a federal grand jury in Birmingham. That rumor turned out not to be a rumor.

At the time they gave their testimony, Sam Gilmore was serving time on federal distilling charges stemming from the 1956 still raid that my father helped carry out.

Well, at least we learned one thing that had gone on behind the scenes. Now that the election was over, the bigger picture, that is, the feds' goal and perhaps that of the Gilmore brothers, was beginning to emerge.

That goal, it became clear a bit later, was not just to sway the election but to put my dad behind bars in a federal prison.

The other shoe dropped hard on Wednesday morning, September 3, 1958, when my dad answered the phone in the sheriff's office. On the other end was U.S. Marshall P. E. Dodd. He delivered the message we feared was imminent. My father had been indicted by a federal grand jury in Birmingham. He was charged with engaging in an illegal liquor conspiracy with the Gilmore brothers according to the testimony of the Gilmore brothers themselves.

Area newspapers reported the indictment under bold front-page headlines. The paper I had worked for, *The Decatur Daily*, ran an inch-high headline across the top of the front page: "U.S. JURY INDICTS LAWRENCE SHERIFF." As a former reporter, I knew the story demanded big play. As a son, it hurt deeply.

We had hoped the grand jury would not indict, but it did, and my dad prepared to fight hard against the charges. He hired Russell Lynne, a relatively high-profile attorney in Decatur. Also hired was a man my father had absolute confidence in. He was R. L. (Bob) Almon of Moulton. Bob Almon was the Matlock of his day, low-key, grounded in common sense, astute in every phase of the law. You underestimated Bob Almon at your own peril. He would not be caught up in the minutia of the moment. He always kept his eye on the bigger prize: acquittal.

Lynne would be out front in the trial defense. He was a small man with quick movements. He was mentally sharp, experienced, and knew how to bore into a prosecution witness. But it was Almon who, behind the scenes, could offer valuable advice on strategy. Almon was noted for his skill in picking a jury too. My dad would have excellent representation.

At 11 a.m. the day after Dodd's call, my dad, accompanied by Lynne, voluntarily surrendered to the U.S. magistrate's office in Birmingham. He was fingerprinted and pleaded "not guilty" before U.S. Commissioner Louise Carlton. He was freed on $500 bond. He would remain in office since there had yet been no conviction.

The grand jury's indictment was based solely on the Gilmore brothers' testimony. The language of the indictment was stiff and legalistic and long. What it said was that Sam Gilmore had agreed to pay Dad $400 a month, at my dad's request, for protection for an illegal distillery. The indictment alleged that Sam Gilmore had told my dad where his stills were, and that my dad had instructed Harold Gilmore, then a deputy, "to let Sam Gilmore know if he saw federal agents in Lawrence County." The grand jury also said that on one occasion my dad conspired to move some barrels of whiskey reputedly owned by Sam Gilmore.

We were perplexed. If all that had occurred, then why weren't the two ex-deputies charged if, as the grand jury found, they conspired with my dad on the payoffs? The more than obvious implication was that a deal had been struck with the feds in return for their testimony. No big surprise there. "Deals" were a common strategy by the feds in cases like this. Our strong suspicion was that the "deal" involved a reduced sentence for Sam Gilmore if my father were convicted.

A few months earlier, Roy Jr. and Harold had gone to *The Decatur Daily* newsroom to complain about a news story that said they had been fired. The paper said the two claimed they had not been fired and "hinted" that they had quit because they did not agree with "certain activities" of the sheriff.

What activities? They could have been referring to any of the several rumors circulating over the county, though they would not say what the "certain activities" were. If they were talking about payoffs, and since no other evidence of any other payoff was included in the indictment, did that mean, if the charges were true, that they objected to my father taking payoffs from their brother? And if there were other payoffs – and surely as deputies they would have known if there had been – why was there no mention of other crimes in the grand jury's report or in the trial that followed?

Such was the reasoning around the jail kitchen breakfast table. Could it be that we were just looking, hoping, for a silver lining in the cloud that hung over us?

We were heartened only a little by Lynne's statement following the arraignment that the government's case was weak, that it might never come to trial. We took most of that as lawyer talk and continued to worry.

My dad's reaction to the indictment was straight-forward.

He said following the arraignment:

"I've been charged with conspiring with three of my ex-deputies to violate the Internal Revenue law. These deputies were discharged by me for a good cause. They are not indicted with me and the charges against me are false and based upon the testimony of those deputies given after I released them.

"The trouble apparently started after my aid in arresting Sam Gilmore at a whiskey still in a raid that took place without the knowledge of either of his two brothers who were then deputies.

"The first blast of publicity does, of course, place me in an unfavorable light, but I am not afraid of the truth."

The front-page picture in *The Decatur Daily* showed my father being led by a U. S. marshall to the arraignment.

The first thing we noticed about the picture was that the knot in his tie fit snugly at the neck. It was a sad sight to see your father being escorted like a common criminal. But while we might have wanted to cry we had to smile just a bit about the tie. Maybe this was a good omen. He hated ties, and when he did wear them, he'd leave them loose at the neck. His portrait is among those of past sheriffs hanging in the foyer of the new Lawrence County Jail. Look closely and you will notice that the knot lacks just a hair being tight at the neck. I don't know that he ever did learn to tie a knot for his ties. When I would come home from college I would tie some of his ties and offer to teach him how. He'd just rather I did it, he said. (Just for the record, it was my college roommate, Mack Walker, who taught *me* how to tie a tie.)

The tie was about the only thing we had to smile about.

The trial was set for April 20 in Huntsville.

Attorneys Lynne and Almon would have more than seven months to prepare their case. We had no choice but to put our faith in them – and God.

Chapter 15

And the Verdict Is...

The jury was handed the case at 3 p.m. Nail-biting time had started in earnest.

Monday morning April 20, 1959, broke over the beautiful Tennessee Valley region of north Alabama with promises of another perfect spring day: temperatures in the 70s with gentle breezes.

Our family had little interest in the weather, however, as we solemnly made our way east over forty miles of highway en route to Huntsville. We stoically stared at fields crawling with tractors and farm machinery as they worked to get another cotton crop into the rich red soil of Limestone and Madison counties.

As it had done last year and the year before and every year before that, the coming of spring awakened the soul to new life, new beginnings, new optimism. I thought of these things as we rolled past the cotton fields and ever closer to that dreaded courtroom. I thought of how our spring this year had been different, darker, less promising. I thought of how lucky those people were driving the tractors and farmers whose only worry on this day was how much cottonseed they could bury.

I was scared, scared for my dad, scared for mom, and scared for my sister. Within the hour we would enter a place where my dad would be put on trial for alleged participation in an illegal liquor conspiracy with three former deputies. What happened in that courtroom in the next two days would determine whether my dad would go to prison, and whether our family would have to suffer for it too, knowing that our most wrenching worry would be for him.

The government charged in the indictment that my father had taken protection money from a former deputy, Sam Gilmore, to allow him to operate an illegal moonshine distillery.

Now the moment of truth had arrived, or at least the attempt to uncover it had arrived. As a news reporter I had covered criminal court trials. I was familiar with courtroom procedure, and I thought if we could just survive the prosecution's opening guns we might have a chance to walk out of the courtroom with our heads high. My fear was that the government had a much stronger case than we knew about, that the prosecution would throw surprises at us that would turn everything around.

Those were my thoughts as federal judge H. H. Grooms called the court into session on that spring morning fifty years ago. At the government's table was U.S. attorney W. L. Longshore, the prosecutor. He looked to be middle-aged and had the look of a seasoned veteran. He looked confident. At the defense table sat my dad, in dark suit and tie (tightened snugly at the neck), and his attorneys, Russell Lynne and R. L. Almon. I was happy to see they looked pretty cool too.

The trial in the Northern District Court of Alabama was held in the U.S. Post Office building. I remember the courtroom as dark and foreboding.

In the witness room waited Sam Gilmore, escorted to the trial from prison, and his brothers Roy Jr. and Harold.

With the preliminaries out of the way, the U.S. prosecutor called them in one by one. Each testified as he had to the federal grand jury in Birmingham the previous

September. Yes, Sam Gilmore agreed to pay my dad $400 a month as protection money for his distillery, they testified. Yes, my dad had taken two months' pay, they said.

Moreover, Sam Gilmore said he had offered my dad $300 a month but that my dad wanted $400. And they implied that my dad conspired to move several barrels of whiskey that allegedly belonged to Sam Gilmore. This was the gist of their testimony. No one to testify to those allegations except them. No surprises. Nothing different. No mention of any other payoffs.

So the first day ended without a bombshell. We headed home that night asking ourselves: "Is that all they've got?" Still, we knew juries were unpredictable, no matter what the evidence showed. We were a little nervous too because we knew that federal agents would be on the stand for the prosecution when the trial resumed the next day.

We traveled back to Huntsville on Tuesday with the threat of severe thunderstorms throughout the afternoon. Could this be one of those ill winds that blows no good?

Inside the courtroom, federal agent James Lusk took the stand for the prosecution. He had been a member of the ill-fated October 1956 raiding party.

Under cross-examination, Lynne asked Lusk if my dad had been cooperative with the federal agents during his term as sheriff. He said that my father had never refused to help the agents and that my father had been an effective moonshine fighter.

Longshore wanted to know if moonshining had started to come back in the county during my dad's second term. Yes, Lusk said.

And while the sheriff may have always cooperated with the agents, had he ever volunteered information? No, the agent replied. Federal agent Cecil Kent offered essentially the same testimony.

As I sat in the courtroom, I was thinking, *This is pretty mild stuff. The agents almost seem to have become a witness for my dad.*

And then on came W. L. "Son" Terry to the stand for the prosecution. What could he add to the case? Terry, of Courtland, the colorful and talkative longtime law enforcement official, testified that Sam Gilmore had asked him in 1957 to ask my dad to return the money he had paid the sheriff. That was strange. Sam Gilmore asked Terry to ask my dad to return money? Sam Gilmore, if he had been serious, couldn't do that himself? Was this a planned maneuver for use later, say in a conspiracy trial?

So what did my dad have to say when Terry relayed the request? "Tell him to pop his whip," my dad said, according to Terry.

The prosecution rested at mid-morning. Next up: the defense.

My dad was sworn in as a witness at 10:30 a.m. He would be there for an hour. And except for five character witnesses he would be the only witness for the defense. I must say, I was proud of him. He came across as cool, collected, and honest, quite a contrast from some of the earlier witnesses.

He recounted his firing of the two deputies some three weeks after he had helped raid Sam Gilmore's still.

My dad said he told the two deputies, "I won't need you any longer." That conversation, he said, took place beside the county jail in Moulton. He said that Highway Patrolman John Brom and my mom were just inside the jail in the sheriff's living quarters.

My dad said the deputies threatened him at that time, saying, "You --- -- - -----, you get out on the road tonight and we will get you."

Lynne asked: Did you enter into an agreement with Sam Gilmore?

My dad answered as if he'd been waiting for this moment to say on the record: "No siree!"

The question of the whiskey barrels was never resolved. Apparently it was brought up by the prosecution to create doubt in the jurors' minds. Here's how my dad explained it. He and Rogersville policeman J. R. Dutton had been watching four barrels of moonshine near Town Creek for most of the day during a heavy rainstorm, hoping the owner would come to pick them up, at which time he would be arrested. Dutton left at 3 p.m.; my father stayed until 6 and returned to Moulton. He sent Roy Gilmore Jr. and Harold Gilmore back to the stakeout at 8 p.m. They came back at 9 and said the whiskey had been moved. Dad answered the obvious question: No, he didn't move the barrels nor did he have anyone else do it.

In answer to the agent's statement that moonshining was again growing in the county, he said he had always been an energetic fighter against moonshine whiskey, that he and his deputies had destroyed a thousand stills and jailed two hundred to three hundred moonshiners during his two terms as sheriff.

Five character witnesses testified to his reputation for honesty. These five people remain on our family's gold star list of devoted friends. They stood with us when a lot of others didn't. Taking the stand on Dad's behalf were state criminal investigator Maurice Chambers, state legislative representative Bruce Dodd of Moulton, neighboring Cullman County Sheriff W. C. Waldrep, Courtland businessman Yancey Hughes, and state parole and probation supervisor Kenneth Tucker. "You can believe what he says," was the essence of their testimony.

The defense rested at noon. Closing arguments would come after lunch. Then the case would go to the jury. We hoped we would have a verdict before nightfall.

The closing arguments took only a few minutes.

Prosecutor Longshore said of the character witnesses' testimony that many a man of good character had been known to change and commit crime.

"Judas was proved of good character the night before he betrayed Christ for thirty pieces of silver," Longshore told the jury.

Lynne, in his closing remarks, declared "the prosecution stems from one thing and one thing only...vengeance," referring to my dad's involvement in arresting Sam Gilmore. And then Lynne too quoted the Bible: "Vengeance is mine, saith the Lord."

Judge Grooms took just twenty minutes to charge the jury; that is, to explain the laws that applied to the case.

The jury was handed the case at 3 p.m. Nail-biting time had started in earnest. We decided not to leave the courtroom for the time being though we figured we would go out for dinner and then go home if the jury had retired for the night. We fully expected the jury to report the next day. That would mean another trip to Huntsville, more time to sweat, and perhaps a restless night.

We had just gotten comfortable in our seats when word came that the jury had reached a decision. The time was 4:45. The jury had deliberated just one hour and forty-five minutes. Good sign or bad? We waited for the announcement.

"The jury finds Franklin P. Smith not guilty."

We were overjoyed to hear the verdict but wondered why the government never got his name right, even in the indictment. Just to correct the record: It's James Franklin Smith.

And just to complete the record as to *The Decatur Daily's* reporting on the acquittal, the paper whose editors and owners taught me as a cub reporter to be fair and objective did not disappoint. The *Daily* gave it the same play they had done for the indictment. The headline in large letters across the top of the front page read: "EX-LAWRENCE SHERIFF IS ACQUITTED."

At long last, the storm clouds that had begun gathering on October 4, 1956, had now parted. The sun was shining, no matter how unstable the weather was that afternoon in Huntsville. My dad had been cleared. The newspapers spoke of how little time it took for the jury to reach a decision. We took satisfaction in the quick verdict.

"A great load has been lifted from my head," Dad told reporters before leaving the courthouse. "I never lost faith. I knew I was innocent and I think most people who know me thought so, too."

What were his feelings now about his former deputies?

"I have no ill will against them," he said. "I believe they were led along into something I honestly don't believe they wanted to do."

Fifty years later I am reminded of this remark by Abraham Lincoln, which puts into perspective this whole painful episode in the lives of my father and our family.

"If the end brings me out all right, what is said against me won't amount to anything. If the end brings me out wrong then ten angels swearing I was right won't make any difference."

For my mom and dad, it was now on to the next phase of their lives. They could now go back to their new home with uplifted hearts. Spring was now spring again. There was a house to furnish, pictures to hang, flowers to plant, a time to breathe deeply the freshness of an April morning. There were chickens to feed and horses to ride and cows to look after and that red Ford tractor just sitting there waiting to be started.

Finally, a little peace had settled into their lives, and a couple of grandchildren to spoil would soon be on the way.

Life would be beautiful, at least for a little while.

Chapter 16

Bright Spring, Dark Winter

His life was full of fateful twists and turns...

With the trial over, Mom and Dad moved on with their lives. The court verdict had unshackled them from the ugly rumors, now no more than fading wisps from a once raging fire.

A little more than two years before, my dad had started preparing for the day he would no longer be sheriff. He began looking for a small farm near Moulton on which he could tend a few cows and a horse or two, a place he could feel again the dirt in his hands and take in the soul-satisfying aroma of freshly plowed soil. He wouldn't be wearing a badge, but any place with a few cows, a few horses, and a few acres of land would do just fine. He would almost be back home in Mt. Hope, doing again what he loved.

He found the perfect spot, thirty-five acres just east of Moulton and almost within the city limits. He closed the deal on January 17, 1957. His first job was to tear down an old house on the property and use some of the lumber to build a small four-room home that his newlywed daughter Patsy and new son-in-law Wyckoff Terry would move into.

Then he had the little farm plowed up and planted in grass for pastureland. Eventually, he would have a dozen or so purebred horned Hereford cows. The brick home for him and Mom was completed in 1958, after his bid for a third term fell short. He did a lot of the work himself on the house, using carpentry and masonry skills he had learned at Mt. Hope.

**Dad was never happier than when he was
astride one of his horses.**

Then within six months of his leaving office on January 19, 1959, Alabama Commissioner of Agriculture A. W. Todd asked if he were interested in becoming a state livestock theft investigator. If the call to inform him of his indictment was the worst he had ever received, then this one must have been one of the best.

He would work primarily in north Alabama, which meant he would spend few nights away from home. His partner, Joe Scott, would become a trusted, close friend. His immediate boss at the state capitol in Montgomery, W. H.

(Mutt) Gregory, could not have been more supportive. It was the ideal job that soothed the wounds of his last two years in the sheriff's office. He had a chance to work with sheriffs he had known before. He loved his work, and the department did too, as evidenced by letters of commendation from Commissioner Todd.

In the meantime he built a 5,000-hen-capacity house to produce eggs. He had added a hog lot, bought his Hereford cows, the Ford tractor, and a one-ton International truck. He hired Joe Owens of Moulton to help run his farm operation while he was out running down cattle rustlers.

Now a state livestock theft investigator, Dad still had time see that his laying hens had fresh sawdust on their floor.

His two loves, farming and law enforcement, had come together to form a career he could only have dreamed of as he sat in that witness chair in a Huntsville courtroom.

Was this a dream too good to be true?

It was.

Among the few bright spots in Dad's final years were two grandsons, Todd, being held here, and Mike.

The man who had overcome every sling and arrow that life had thrown at him was about to face the deadliest one of all.

The call came to me at Auburn from Wyckoff in late 1961. My dad had been diagnosed with some sort of blood disease, and the doctors hadn't figured out exactly what it was. We were hoping that it was nothing serious.

His local family doctor, Dr. Robert Rhyne, later diagnosed the problem as lymphoma – in broad laymen's terms, a form of leukemia. But he had not been able to get a confirmation from the lab. Still a little hope, we thought. Lab tests at the University of Alabama at Birmingham Hospital ended all doubts. My dad suffered from adult acute lymphoblastic leukemia, a cancer of the blood in which the bone marrow produces too many white blood cells.

This trying time brought two new names to our family's list of heroes. One was Commissioner Todd, who made arrangements for my dad to visit Ochsner Clinic in New Orleans for tests and treatment. That was just one of many gestures of kindness and support he gave our family. The other is Dr. Rhyne, who stayed at Dad's side, offered encouragement, and demonstrated a caring concern at every turn. Our family remains eternally grateful to both.

The decline in Dad's health was slow but certain. He was continually in and out of the local hospital for drug treatments; often Dr. Rhyne would have to drain fluid from his lungs.

I don't recall him ever complaining about his condition. Patsy and Wyckoff never could either. Wyckoff became especially close to Dad during these dark days. They spent a lot of time together, Wyckoff helping with the cows, working with him on jobs around the farm. He said Dad fought the disease without complaint, never asked "Why me?" and never stopped looking to the future. That's the way it seemed when I visited, but I thought perhaps that was just an act for my sake. It wasn't. He had a gritty, bulldog determination, my dad, and I think, as does Wyckoff, that until the very last he felt he would eventually overcome another of life's obstacles, just as he had done so many times before.

He continued to lose weight and strength though. His home became a cot loaned to him by my in-laws, Ernest and Hilda Shelton. Aside from letting me marry their daughter, Martha, they were among our closest friends and supporters.

Mr. Shelton, a legendary political figure himself in Lawrence County, served five six-year terms as circuit clerk.

Mom set the cot in the den, placed so Dad could put his head on a pillow to watch television. He hadn't been able to work for weeks. His supervisors told him not to worry, just get well. He was thin, weak-voiced, a shell of his former self. I hugged him and felt his love through the scratchy whiskers on his gaunt face. Except when he held me as a baby, this was the first time we had ever hugged.

That moment of shared feeling as he lay decimated on the cot that day was a tremendously emotional moment for me, and I suspect it was for him. We both tried not to show it. As Martha and I drove back to Auburn, I had the feeling I had seen my father alive for the last time.

Amazingly, he rallied. He gained weight and strength, and just as amazing, he went back to work. Had he turned the corner? Would he be able to fight his way out of another dilemma? We were almost afraid to hope. The three-day monthly drug treatments provided by Ochsner Clinic and administered by Dr. Rhyne seemed to be having a positive effect. Recovery from each of those treatments took another couple of days and then, after he had summoned up the strength to drive, he would head out again to somewhere in north Alabama hunting the culprits who had stolen pigs or horses or cows from an unsuspecting farmer.

On December 18, 1964, three years after the first symptoms appeared, he went to the hospital for the final time. A day or so before, in extraordinarily raw weather that can invade Alabama in December, he had gone outside to feed his cows. He stayed out too long and developed pneumonia, which is often the "complication" that causes the death of weakened leukemia sufferers.

Christmas Eve night 1964 descended on the little town of Moulton with a quiet sadness, at least for our family. Around the town square, Christmas lights twinkled peacefully from street light posts. Darkness had settled in on the few shoppers searching for last-minute gifts. Traffic was light. The town would soon be putting itself to bed, awaiting another Christmas Day of toys and food and joyous family gatherings.

Three blocks off the square, in room 158 of Lawrence County Hospital, my father clung precariously to life. Pneumonia had caused his kidneys to quit functioning three days before. The end was near. Friends and family gathered at his bedside.

The man who for a lifetime struggled to show his emotions asked for a pencil and paper.

He began laboriously to scrawl barely readable block letters...

I L O V E

He stopped, too tired to continue. He motioned for my mother to take the note.

"You know what I mean?" he pleaded with his eyes as much as with a voice that had weakened to a whisper.

She nodded yes and began crying. She clasped the note. It would become a lifetime treasured possession.

"I'm ready to go," he said, looking up at my mother. She kissed him on the forehead and bade him goodbye.

Minutes later, at exactly 8 p.m., my father quietly breathed his last. He was fifty-three.

When you reach the mid-seventies, as I have, fifty-three seems such a short life. But during those fifty-three years he demonstrated his strength of character in so many ways, and in many ways we probably never learned about. His life was full of fateful twists and turns, but he always found a way not just to overcome but to come back stronger than before.

He wasn't supposed to have lived when that two-by-four hit him in the head when it came flying off a sawmill belt, but he did.

He wasn't supposed to win an election for sheriff, this unknown carpenter-mason from Mt. Hope, but he did.

He wasn't much of a politician, they said, but at one point he was the most popular politician in the county. He wouldn't bounce back from those vile rumors, they said, but he did. The trial would end his career in law enforcement, some said, but it didn't.

My dad's old friend, Limestone County Sheriff M. W. (Buddy) Evans, called him "a man of courage" who "never complained a minute" about his illness. Columnist Winford Turner of *The Decatur Daily* described him as "one of the best lawmen to ever put on a badge in this area."

My mother had demonstrated her own brand of courage, both before and after my dad's death. She never bowed to the pressures of running the first floor of the jail. She put up with a lot during her oftentimes topsy-turvy jail home. She was more than willing to accept the challenge and more than adequate in meeting it. She showered her love on Screwdriver and Joyce and on just about anybody else fortunate enough to have been in the presence of her goodness. That included us, her family, who in hindsight were not nearly as appreciative as we should have been.

She may have shown the most courage as she lay bedridden for nine years in a Florence nursing home with an arthritic condition that contorted her body in hideous ways. Yet she never lost her smile, never lost her appreciation for her friends and family, never stopped believing in her husband. She never stopped believing in angels, nor in the power of prayer.

And never did she fear death. She looked forward to the day when God would say to her, "Ruby, it's time for you to go meet Franklin."

God's call came at 11:05 p.m., January 16, 2008. She was ninety-five and had suffered enough. After forty-four years, she and that man whose pale blue eyes she always thought were so beautiful were united once again.

There are no monuments to their time on this earth, except for Franklin Smith Road, for which I'm sure my dad would have been proud. No gold watch retirement dinners.

They lived and they died.

With the passage of time, my mom and dad's eight years in the sheriff's office have become for later generations no more than a footnote in history. But their life mattered. It mattered to us, the family, and it mattered to a lot of other people in Lawrence County during that decade of long ago.

Their legacy to us, their family, is one of courage and commitment and perseverance, leaning on Christian principles through good times and bad, and all of that without rancor toward those who may have wished them ill.

May those of us who survive carry that legacy in our hearts as well, and pass it to our children and our grandchildren, and to their children and beyond. That is their legacy to Patsy and me, to Mike and Todd, to Suzanne, to Reagan and Ruby, to Maggie and Claire. That legacy is the only monument they would have cared about anyway.

Mom and Dad are at peace now, laid to rest side by side in Moulton Memory Gardens.

May God rest their souls.

The End

LaVergne, TN USA
16 October 2009
161183LV00001B/2/P